Stan Grant is a Wiradjuri and Kamilaroi man. A journalist since 1987, he has worked for the ABC, SBS, the Seven Network and Sky News Australia. From 2001 to 2012 he worked for CNN as an anchor and senior correspondent in Asia and the Middle East. As a journalist, he has received a string of prestigious international and Australian awards. In 2015, he published his bestselling book *Talking to My Country*, which won the Walkley Book Award, and he also won a Walkley Award for his coverage of Indigenous affairs. In 2016 he was appointed to the Referendum Council on Indigenous recognition. Stan is now Chair of Indigenous/Australian Belonging at Charles Sturt University and International Affairs Analyst at the ABC.

Also by Stan Grant
and published by HarperCollins

Talking to My Country

Australia Day

With the Falling of the Dusk

The Queen is Dead

Tears of Strangers

Stan Grant

Tears of Strangers

Stan Grant

HarperCollinsPublishers

HarperCollins*Publishers*
Australia • Brazil • Canada • France • Germany • Holland • India
Italy • Japan • Mexico • New Zealand • Poland • Spain • Sweden
Switzerland • United Kingdom • United States of America

HarperCollins acknowledges the Traditional Custodians
of the land upon which we live and work, and pays respect
to Elders past and present.

First published in Australia in 2002
This edition published in 2023
by HarperCollins*Publishers* Australia Pty Limited
Gadigal Country
Level 19, 201 Elizabeth Street, Sydney NSW 2000
ABN 36 009 913 517
harpercollins.com.au

HarperCollins Publishers
Macken House, 39/40 Mayor Street Upper
Dublin 1, D01 C9W8, Ireland

A catalogue record for this book is available from the National Library of Australia

ISBN 978 1 4607 6532 6 (paperback)
ISBN 978 0 7304 9154 5 (ebook)

Cover design by Louise McGeachie, adapted by HarperCollins Design Studio
Goanna illustration by Max and Gloria Reid
Author photograph by Kathy Luu
Typeset in Sabon by Kirby Jones
Printed and bound in Australia by McPherson's Printing Group

MIX
Paper | Supporting responsible forestry
FSC® C001695
FSC www.fsc.org

For my father — my hero

I saw the tears of the oppressed —
and they have no comforter;
Power was on the side of their oppressors —
and they have no comforter.

Ecclesiastes 4:1

The tears of strangers are nothing
but water.

Russian proverb

Contents

Introduction

I have spent most of my life . . . watching white people and outwitting them so that I might survive.

JAMES BALDWIN, *NOBODY KNOWS MY NAME*

The scene is Sydney's five-star Westin Hotel. Four hundred people have paid $220 a head to reconcile their differences. There's a former prime minister and his equally famous partner; at least three federal politicians, including the current Leader of the Opposition; an internationally famous actor; assorted television and radio stars; models; and a Booker Prize winning author. They sit next to Aboriginal bureaucrats, Aboriginal athletes and Aboriginal singers, black dancers, actors, lawyers and the former head of the Aboriginal and Torres Strait Islander Commission.

Over a three-course meal washed down with expensive bottles of wine, they lament the lack of a national apology to Aborigines for crimes of the past. The women rattle their jewellery and powder their noses, while the men check their cuff links and straighten their bow ties. As I step up to the podium to welcome them, I can't help being struck by how vaguely obscene this is. Only the day before I had sat with my cousin as he drank himself into a stupor. He's lived at the coalface of Australian racism: opportunities denied, insults freely given. He's spent a lifetime looking down. He has the body of a man twice his age and his memory is lost in an alcoholic haze. These people were here to save him? To reconcile on his behalf? Two hundred and twenty dollars, the cost of a place here, would buy him enough food for a month, or enough booze to forget.

Not only was this scene incongruous, it also reeked of a smugness that passed itself off as sincerity. I asked every white person in the room to stand up. They fidgeted and looked uncomfortable.

'Would anyone who has shared a Christmas dinner with an Aborigine please sit down,' I said.

No more than half a dozen people resumed their seats. The others were frozen with the realisation that they could be exposed.

'Anyone who is related to an Aborigine please sit down.'

Again there was a nervous shuffling of feet but almost everyone remained standing.

'Anyone whose children have invited Aboriginal friends home to play please sit down.'

I'd made my point. The relief was palpable as everyone chuckled at the irony. Yes, we had a long way to go.

But the same questions could have been asked of many of the blacks present. How many of them were living comfortably in white suburbia? How many were like chameleons, pulling on the cloak of blackness only when it suited them? How many, like me, were living with white partners in comfortable homes with children in private schools? We called ourselves Aborigines, but I was unsure of what that meant any more. What, I asked myself, did I have in common with a black petrol-sniffing teenager from Yuendumu?

According to the current definition of 'Aborigine', a mostly white Sydney suburban teenager for whom the Dreamtime exists only in fiction can share an identity with the sons of Namatjira. Similarly a family falling-out, in theory, could see a tribally initiated man denied recognition of his Aboriginality. People who have lived as white Australians, oblivious to black ancestry, can discover a long-lost Aboriginal great-great-grandparent and claim to be Aborigines themselves. One well-known artist, whose family deny they're Aborigines, is known to return periodically to her tribal homeland and strip naked to run in the bush and connect with her spiritual past.

As I looked out at the audience at the Westin Hotel I saw people who, except for the shade of their skin, looked little different from their white guests. They decry assimilation, while all the facts of their lives say otherwise. Is Aboriginal identity means-tested? Of course not, but as I thought of my cousin and compared his life — and the lives of so many Aborigines — with mine, I couldn't help but feel my success somehow mocked him.

I live in a country where black is not a word, it's a sentence. Black boys fry their brains with petrol fumes. Black children starve to death in flyblown camps surrounded by drunks, drugs and disease. Black women have their guts kicked out by emotionally castrated black men. Three-year-old black girls are raped by their fathers, brothers and uncles. Blacks fill up the prisons and the graveyards. They don't work and they die of dysentery and leprosy.

I've escaped that world; no, not escaped it, abandoned it. Their misery doesn't need my company. They choke the life out of me with fear and shame. They reek of death and danger and of a violence that terrifies the white in me. I scurry back to the shelter of my acceptably brown skin. I've long ago paid the last instalment on the price of my affluence and assimilation.

I live in a country where black is not a word, it's a privilege. I'm not supposed to say that. I'm supposed to chant that statistical mantra that places me amongst the most impoverished and oppressed peoples on earth. I'm supposed to sit looking out at the ocean from my house on one of the richest strips of real estate in Australia and tell white people they owe me. In Australia, black leaders — self-styled saviours of the oppressed — know the value of a good bottle of red and the lease payments on a Mercedes or BMW. In Australia, black actor Ernie Dingo can do tourism advertisements urging Australians to 'Go on, see Australia!' with no hint of irony. Black athlete Cathy Freeman can appear in sports commercials on TV making a pun on the word 'sorry', a word that so many of her people so desperately need to hear from whites. Anthony Mundine can arrive at a boxing bout in a red Ferrari draped in a red, black and yellow Aboriginal flag and dub himself the 'original Aboriginal'. I live in a country where being an Aborigine is a marketing tool.

I stand at a crucial moment in Aboriginal history. Our challenge is no longer solely from without, but equally from within. Aboriginal identity today is fractured, lacerated by class, gender and geography in ways we've never before seen. Our identity as Aborigines is as problematic as personal choice, and the bonds of injustice and poverty no longer apply. It's a mockery to talk of black unity, as it is to reject white people. Whiteness abounds in ways we can't even — or maybe don't want to — see. We deny the obvious to maintain our often dubious identities.

Expressing our blackness exposes our hypocrisy. Australia has us trapped in its pervasive whiteness. We embrace our success, enjoy its trappings with a feigned contempt, while taking for granted the comfort of a full stomach and warm bed. We haven't yet learnt to identify ourselves beyond the prism of poverty. We have a perverse longing, a lingering attachment to the injustice and oppression that we imagine nourish our identity. Shamelessly, we compete for victim status and turn pain and loss into virtues.

White Australia, our perceived enemy, has become our greatest ally. It engages in what sociologists call an 'imperialist nostalgia': the lament for the loss of a culture it helped destroy. Australia is recreating Aboriginal society as it imagines it should be; it's a blackness seen through white eyes and offers blacks something to believe in, or even cash in on. But it offers no freedom, simply subservience. We have moved beyond the fact of race and arrived at race as a concept. We are chained to the predictability of Aboriginal identity by a laziness that fails to grapple with our inconsistencies and fraudulence; we remain perplexed by our very existence.

The old definitions of Aboriginality no longer adequately serve the range of contending groups that lay claim to a black identity in Australia. No-one can be denied an identity; each person is entitled to express their self-image. Similarly the construction of that identity cannot go unexamined. It's a process already under way in the United States and long overdue here. As American writer Manning Marable says in his book *Beyond Black and White*:

> We have entered a period in which our traditional definitions of what it has meant to be 'black' must be transformed. The old racial bifurcation of white versus black no longer accurately or adequately describes the social composition and ethnic character of the United States.

The answer lies in a true understanding of our history. Not the lies and distortions of history woven to suit a political agenda. It requires us to free ourselves of orthodoxy, white and black, to examine our motives and actions critically. George Orwell wrote in his novel *1984*, 'He who controls the present owns the past; he who owns the past controls the future.' At this moment, for Aborigines, Orwell's warning has never appeared more urgent or prophetic. We have never truly owned our story; we've always been defined and interpreted by a white society that imposed British law and structures upon us, deemed us British subjects, then excluded us and exploited us.

Aboriginal 'culture' has grown out of our struggle to maintain our separate identity in the overpowering presence of white Australia. Our 'culture' now is represented in a mish-mash of residual hostility to white settlement, a deep, lingering sense of injustice, socioeconomic inequity and a romantic attachment to perceived artefacts and rituals of our imagined cultural past. We lay claim to a homogeneity and unity that never existed in our pre-settlement societies. Mixed-blood, detribalised Aborigines from the southern cities look longingly to the Northern Territory and Western Australia to regain the traditions they believe they've lost.

Art, film, music and dance have drawn on the convergence of the disparate elements of Aboriginal societies to fashion an identity that gives us a sense of ourselves as unique and distinct. The Aboriginal political struggle has exposed and smashed prejudice and discrimination. It has fostered a burgeoning pride in Aboriginal heritage. But we must destroy the logic and the language of inequality and inferiority. Black society is forever changing. An immutable, homogeneous Aboriginal identity is untenable. As there is no permanence to blackness, white society cannot be seen exclusively as one of power and privilege.

For every middle-class Aborigine who appropriates the pain of his long-suffering 'brothers and sisters', there is a group of Aborigines still condemned to a life of poverty, neglect and hopelessness. Do I have the same claim on social justice as more disadvantaged blacks? Certainly not. We share a common historical experience, and in some cases a cultural and even a family bond, but our circumstances have transformed a purely racial solidarity. So many Aborigines have fashioned themselves in the image of their conquerors and comfort themselves with a convenient cultural and historical revisionism. In the words of African–American writer Michael Eric Dyson in *Reflecting Black*, 'we must transcend the gaze of race and look to a more ecumenical constellation of forces — age, gender and class among them'.

There are obvious challenges for government policies aimed at an egalitarian outcome for all Australians regardless of colour. But my aim here is not to devise political solutions, but to ask the hard questions. Who am I? Who are my people? Aboriginal lives have been smashed against Australia's whiteness for over 200 years. Yet we've reached out, trying to find a way to live together and share this land. My people's lives need to be treated with tenderness, but concern for the future means throwing off sentiment for clear-eyed analysis. In my search for my own truth, I'm inspired by the words of another great black writer, Toni Morrison: 'My work requires me to think about how free I can be as an African-American woman writer in my genderised, sexualised, wholly racialised world.'

Part of this search means unlocking secrets, always painful and often tragic. I hesitate now as I stare at a blank page that I know will soon reveal perhaps more than I would like it to. But the truth demands courage. I hope only one thing: that one day Aborigines can be free of the all too often painful choices our blackness has forced upon us.

1

My Father's Son

. . . no-one is such a coward that he could not be inspired into courage by love and made the equal of someone who's naturally very brave.

PLATO, *SYMPOSIUM*

My father's name is Stan, and I'm named after him. Strangely, or maybe not, I've never felt comfortable with that name; it's just never quite fitted me. Dad calls me Dylan; others call me Gug. Maybe Dad never wanted me to have his name in the first place. Anyway, he wasn't there when I was born so he didn't have much choice. Mum named me because Dad was nowhere to be seen. Hours she waited for him at the hospital, watched as other dutiful husbands revelled in their new families. Dad was locked up. He and Crow Williams had been out celebrating. I don't know the details but there was too much grog, two blackfellas and a broken shop window. We got off on the wrong foot and have somehow struggled to get in step ever since.

Prison, or 'boob', or 'the peter', as Dad called it, had become a pattern for him. No long stretches, but enough short stints to add up. There'd been a prima facie case against Dad from the time he was born. The vagaries of biology meant that he couldn't find an alibi in racial ambiguity like others in his family. They called my father 'Black Horse' for a reason. In the racially charged 1950s and 1960s, black skin was too often proof of a crime. Drinking wasn't a crime, being black and drinking was; swearing was acceptable, black swearing was offensive language; being poor was no crime, being black and poor meant a man could lose his family or his home. This was the world Dad lived in, and he has the scars to prove it.

The story of my father's life is written on his body. By the time I was old enough to understand, he'd learnt to laugh at his pain. He'd tell me how he'd been bashed, poisoned, stabbed, had almost every bone in his body broken and been shot at into the bargain. His 'boong' nose had been exaggerated by too many fists to the face in too many two-quid-a-night tent-boxing scraps. When he was a teenager in Redfern a crazed Greek café owner aimed a carving knife at Dad's throat, which ended up sticking out of his left shoulder. The Greek got a kicking, and my father is left with the scar from a wound that healed itself in the back alleys around Eveleigh Street.

In my child's eye Dad is sitting in a bath, the water turned black from blood and sap. His eyes are closed as if he's willing the hot water to wash away the dull pain from his muscles. A warm bath was about as much luxury as a sawmiller could afford. Day after day Dad would lump logs three times his size at any mill where he could find work. Sawmills are peopled by a strange breed of men who measure their survival on the stumps that once were fingers; each one a mark not of carelessness but of escape. For Dad, not being able to play the guitar any more was a fair trade for feeding his family.

The years of sawmilling stacked muscles on the muscles he'd already built in the boxing tents. Dad used to boast that he could break leather straps just by flexing his biceps. To the muscles and black skin he added a layer of tattoos that made him an even more fearsome figure. These weren't tattoos as art, these were a form of self-mutilation, blue ink carvings scratched out during the endless nights of prison lock-down. Across his chest was my mother's name, Betty; if he flexed his forearms he could make Fred Flintstone chase Barney Rubble; and on his fingers were two names from his past that would eventually collide with my future.

The letter didn't arrive so much as ambush me. It came when I wasn't looking and lay in wait, patiently sitting out my absence. It contained a truth that would last an eternity; it would lose none of its impact by remaining unopened for an extra week. I had been away in Greece on a job, and I found it sitting on my desk when I returned. I don't know that many people can pinpoint the exact moment their life changed; I know I can. From that moment I was free of a lie and had allegiance only to the truth. The truth can hurt or heal; we have the power to decide which. My truth would save me. No more would I lead a weak, inhibited life that valued obligation and duty above freedom. My sensible, responsible self had made me a success, but I'd welcome failure to now embrace recklessness. I would be shackled to my father's darkness no more.

'I don't know if you know about me, my name is Debbie and I'm your sister,' the letter read.

Suddenly it was as though I was the one caught out. I closed the letter like a naughty child shoves a half-eaten packet of biscuits back into the cupboard. But nothing that is opened can be closed again; nothing that is known can be unknown. I didn't for a moment think what I'd read could be a lie. It was true, I instinctively knew that. What I didn't want to know was the truth of the truth. I didn't reopen the letter. I drove home, had my dinner, kissed my children, watched television, went to sleep, woke up — and never for a moment, awake or asleep, had the revelation of my newborn fully grown sister left my mind.

Debbie was married with seven children and living on an Aboriginal reserve on the far north coast of

New South Wales. Her husband was named Stephen and her children Aaron, Eric, Nadine, Tamika, Jimmy, David and Jordan. She was thirty-eight years old; that made her just one year older than me . . . one year to the day, in fact. I was born on 30 September 1963, Debbie on the same day in the same month, 1962. One year in which lives would begin and end and fates be sealed.

There were two other names in the letter: Barbara and Donna. But these I already knew. Barbara and Donna had travelled every road my family had gone down, lived in every house we called home. They ate every meal with us; at night they slept in bed with my mother and father. Barbara and Donna were the names I would never ask about, names Dad had stopped speaking years before, but carried still in his strong, black hands. Barbara and Donna were scratched in ink on my father's skin, along with Betty and Fred and Barney. Now in Debbie's letter they were alive; Barbara as the mother I could have had and Donna as the long dead sister I would never know.

These were the facts of Debbie's life: names, dates, places — but there was something more here. This was a story of the little lives that never make the pages of history. No-one here had turned back armies, plundered nations, led revolutions or righted great wrongs; these people were just grist to time's mill. They were our lost causes and losers, the Australians who don't all rejoice but sing a sadder anthem improvised from broken keys and too many blue notes. Debbie, in a two-page letter, had introduced me to a father I'd never known despite thirty-seven years of living with him.

I'd always been afraid for Dad. There was something in those dark eyes that could burn with rage, yet at other times swim in pools of sadness. I always feared he'd go and never return. Not that he would desert us, but that danger would claim him for its own. It was as though fate had already dug his grave somewhere. I can still feel the knot in my stomach that I felt as a boy as I waited, shaking, for him to come home. I'd squeeze myself up against a window and peer through the curtain, night after night, longing for the first trace of the plume of dust that would tell me his old ute was rattling its way home. It wasn't as though I'd run to the door and greet him with a kiss; we weren't like that. I'd just breathe again, for the first time in hours, it seemed, and rest up in bed for a repeat of the ritual the next day.

I never felt as though Dad liked me; somehow I was too soft for him.

'He's just sensitive, that's all.' Mum's defence of me became part of the problem. Sawmillers' sons don't need defending by their mothers. Every step I took away from him I felt him take two away from me, until we became like two prizefighters who operated out of opposite corners and could only embrace after each battle. He didn't hit me often, but when he did I hated him. My father belted me with all the fury only a black man could muster hitting someone he imagines to be white.

Mostly I'd get the strap, or a thin, whippy, switch off a tree, which he'd get me to fetch. He'd wield them both with a ferocity that would leave me with telltale welts for days. Occasionally I'd get the full force of his fist, a fist that had felled men twice his size. Once he hit me at one end of the kitchen and sent me sprawling the length of the room until I came to rest against the fridge. Like some cartoon character, I was suspended in midair before slowly sliding into a crumpled heap on the floor. I took my last beating from him when I was fifteen. I'd gone for a drive with my cousins without telling him, and when I returned he launched into a rage. He dragged me by the hair into the back of our car and laid into my ribs and back. I don't know whether I refused to speak to him or was genuinely in shock, but hours passed before he came to me with a tenderness and a remorse I'd never seen from him before. He never hit me again.

'I'm sorry,' Dad said. 'I just want us to be mates, that's all.'

If he was looking for absolution I certainly wasn't going to be so generous. I curled up tight as a fist, my eyes staring blankly at the wall ahead.

Dad told me he didn't want me to repeat his mistakes. There was a better life for me in this world. I know now he wanted to tell me more, that his had been a hard life with hard choices. That his survival, our survival, meant carrying no passengers, including his own flesh and blood . . . including Debbie. Now she was doing it for him; in her letter Debbie was saying the things he couldn't say then and still can't today. The fact of her existence, the shadow of a life she'd led, formed Dad's excuse and made his violence somehow understandable. Dad had scrounged up chance's loose change and gambled it all on me. I was his lucky number and he and Debbie and all the rest of my family would have to cut their losses.

I wonder now, though, how many times Dad looked on me with regret. On my birthday, did he also remember his daughter? Nature had played a cruel trick: each 30 September would remind him of what he'd gained and what he'd lost, the life he had and the life he'd left behind. We were lucky, we had him; he fought for us and he fed us. For Debbie he existed only in resentment and loss. For Dad there was the unforgiving struggle between his devotion and his neglect. He dealt with it in silence. Some mornings I'd find him listening to his favourite songs, country songs about lost chances. He found meaning and solace in the mournful lyrics of singers like Merle Haggard.

One year separated me and Debbie, one year and a lifetime. In a year my father had sobered up and straightened out. He put down the bottle, checked his temper and brought his pay packet home. He conquered his demons and he loved us. He wrote a love letter to my mother from jail and then made good on every promise. It was a commitment to live as a whitefella; his blackness had been bashed out of him. If living white's what it took then white's what he'd be.

Like hundreds of displaced blacks Dad had been living on the streets of Sydney's inner-city suburb of Redfern. In a tough world he gave as good as he got, and he got plenty. He never killed a man, but he was close enough. It was a wild brawl and only good luck that it was one of his mates' fists and not his own that sent a man sprawling to the ground, his head splitting open like a ripe watermelon as it hit the concrete. Debbie was born into that violent world; I was part of Dad's escape.

The odd thing is, deep down, my father likes whites; he wants them to like him. His father had taught him that equality came from God. Cecil Grant had fought in Australia's war, lived in whites' houses, sent his kids to their schools and won their respect. As in so many cases, though, assimilation did not survive the town limits. In another city, another era, Cecil Grant's son was just another Abo, a black kid with a smart mouth who needed to be taught a lesson. The black-hating cops in Redfern decided they'd be the ones to do it. Dad never told me about this; I discovered it in a book in a library in Canberra. The book was Faith Bandler's *Time Was Ripe* and in it another Aborigine, Ken Brindle, told me about the father I never knew.

> . . . there was a bloke named Stan Grant from Cowra who got into a little skirmish in front of the Town Hall. The police came down and punched the Christ out of him in front of the place.

> Instead of just arresting him, they gave him a good flogging in front of all the other people. I was on the door that night so I went out and objected. I said: 'There's no need to kick that boy. If you want to arrest him, arrest him and take him and charge him. You don't have to batter him.'

'I found this today, Dad,' I said, when I got home.

He looked at it and read slowly, each word taking him back to a place and a time he'd wanted to shield us from.

'Yeah, they bashed the hell out of us,' he said. No hint of bitterness, just the facts and nothing more.

I'd blamed this man for hitting me . . . hated him for it. But I didn't know. I wanted to say sorry, I wanted to put my arm around him — but there was a distance between us that was too great. Dad had healed himself as best as he could, and I knew now what that hint of sadness was that I'd caught in his eyes. I knew why, as a boy, I'd worried so about him.

My father wasn't brutal; like too many of his generation he was brutalised. It's not right that a young boy is bashed senseless by police; that he gets locked up for 'crimes' a white person would not even be charged for; that he must spend his life wandering from town to town to scrape together enough work to feed his family. Somehow, though, love found its way into that life and I'm here today because my dad truly loved my mum. But he also loved before my mum, and if family meant anything I'd have to meet Debbie, laugh with her and cry with her and see if it was true that blood is thicker than water.

Fire and snow trailed my journey from Sydney to the small Aboriginal mission in northern New South Wales. It was like my personal apocalypse. At Guyra on the New England Highway the air turned bitterly cold and the soft white flakes settled and thickened on my windscreen. It was late August and winter had decided to let out one last sigh before making way for the spring sun. Within half an hour, though, flames leapt from the treetops and scorched the ground as a bushfire swept along the hills that shrouded Debbie's little village. Nature had laid on a fitting welcome for me; it matched my wildly swinging moods over the months since I'd first read my new-found sister's letter.

So much had changed. I had changed. I received Debbie's letter in June and in two months I'd left my job, my wife and home. My new relationship had moved from mere gossip to scandal, plastered in headlines across newspaper front pages. Celebrity left no room for dignity. Many of my so-called friends had betrayed me. I had stopped speaking to my family — my mother and father — and I met Debbie alone.

I'd spoken to my sister — by now I called her Sis — many times in the past few weeks. I recall the first time: I phoned her at work and told the receptionist it was her brother calling. Her brother . . . yes, that is what I was. The voice down the line was comfortingly familiar, it had a sound that I'd long ago stopped hearing.

'Hello,' she said.

Only it wasn't hello, not as I say it, or maybe you. I can't really write it at all, not even phonetically. This was a black voice: a dropped aitch, rounded vowels, a flat cadence with the only hint of melody in the slight upward inflection. That's one way of describing it; I could also say it sounded like home.

There was so much to say, so much to ask, but mostly I just needed to hear her. I needed to hear if there was anything of me in her voice. Maybe there was, maybe it was just the memory of something I'd lost. I called her again that night; now I could taste my homesickness. It was the sound of the onions frying in the background, the kids laughing and running in and out of the house. It was noisy and beautiful and peaceful all at the same time.

I spoke to Debbie often over the next few weeks. She never judged me, she never questioned me. Debbie was the only person truly asking nothing of me. What I, and others — especially others — saw as personal turmoil, Debbie could shrug off with a nonchalance that comes from knowing things can definitely be a whole lot worse. There was always that sound of home in our phone calls; a simpler home that I'd long ago swapped for the grand delusions and superfluous trappings of success. She lived light, and she lived honestly.

Debbie hadn't waited thirty-seven years and then decided to reveal herself to me; she'd tried to see me once before. When she was eighteen she'd travelled to Canberra to meet her father. Dad wasn't ready and decided we weren't ready either. He met his daughter and took her to my grandmother's — our grandmother's — house. Debbie says that Nan took one look at her and recognised her immediately; she'd carried a photo of Debbie, taken as a child, and showed it to her. I suppose it was Nan's way of showing she'd never forgotten her granddaughter. My uncle met her, as did my aunty, but not me. Debbie left the following day, back to her life, leaving us to ours.

I was furious when I found out. My family had put its seal on this silence. Why didn't they tell me? Dad I could understand . . . just. But my nan?

We never really stop being children, do we? We take on adult bodies, adult worries and adult lies, but we can still hurt like babies. That's how I felt then: like a child abandoned. How does a family decide who can or can't be a member? How does an Aboriginal family, which knows the pain of separation, inflict that pain on its own? I was angry then, not now. Now I know that mine was a selfish indignation. I see now that secrets can often be our salvation; they keep out the truth that may otherwise tell us we're no good. Life will eventually expose us, but our secrets at least buy us some time.

Why am I telling you this now? If it was just family business you'd have no more right to mine than I would to yours, but this is bigger than that. This is your story and my story, the story of a country that took black lives and smashed them. It smashed their culture, their language and their families. This is my father's legacy, and the pain I've inherited. It's about what makes us black, even when you don't see it. I don't write this to condemn, but to remove the blindfold of Australia's history to reveal what it's created. I'm telling you this in the hope that in some small way I can make sense of Dad's life, Debbie's life and the countless other lives that have been sacrificed to Australia's unbearable whiteness.

And Debbie was white. More white than black if blood is your guide. She was also blacker than me. Black, in an identity that isn't chosen but totally natural. If I'd had any doubts, then Debbie's face dispelled them in an instant. She was a Grant. She looked more like a Grant than I do. I've inherited my mother's sharp angles; Debbie had the round face, broad, flat nose and high forehead that came from her Wiradjuri ancestors. Her children, too, were hardly strangers: I'd seen their faces all of my life, and Debbie's son, Eric, looked more like his grandfather than any of my kids. There wasn't much of Barbara, her mother, in Debbie's features, not that I could see anyway. I think Barbara was comforted by that – that in her daughter's face there was a reminder of a man she loved.

Somehow I wasn't prepared for Barbara to be white. But it made perfect sense. It told of a world, not so long ago, when black and white were not supposed to love each other. And it told a story of Australia that was more sad and more real than the whitewashed heroics of my schoolboy history books. Barbara was white and when Dad left her he married my mum, the whitest black woman he could find. Australia in the 1960s had laws that were meant to stop this sort of thing. Blacks were divided into fractions: halves, quarters, eighths. We stopped being whole and were known instead as quadroons and octoroons. It was an arbitrary hierarchy of complexion that could be corrupted by spending an extra hour in the summer sun. Where you fitted determined your fate. Barbara's sin was the greatest of all; she slept with a black man and crossed a colour line over which she would never return.

She was old and she was crippled. I wasn't prepared for this either. Multiple sclerosis had robbed her of the independence that had been so hard won, and of which she'd been so proud. She had a face that had long stopped fussing over vanity; what energy she had left she saved for easing her pain and loving her family. The years had been hard and had buried the girl she'd once been. But there were glimpses of her young self still, in her straight talking and her grit that defied her affliction now, as it had defied bigots then.

'They were hard days,' she said.

I just looked on, afraid to disturb her memory; a memory she raked over daily, and was doing so again for me.

'Your father was a boxer . . . didn't use the name Grant, though. He called himself Ellems.'

In the easy flow of Aboriginal families, names were not important; half of Dad's father's family used their mother's name, Ellems.

'Yeah, Stan didn't want his mum knowing he was fighting,' Barbara said.

She told me about the drinker, the brawler and the good man who worked hard and always brought his money home. And she told me about the police.

'They were terrible to your father . . . and me,' she said. 'They used to stop the wagon and drag us off the street if we were walking together . . . they gave him some terrible hidings.'

She told me other things that I won't tell you; things that would do no good for anyone else to know. It ended, Dad married Mum and had me, my brothers and sister. Life happened.

We all make our choices; none of us really knows if they are the right ones, and our choices are often brutal. Dad's choices were limited because he wore a black skin in a country that could see itself only as white. Barbara's life, too, was limited by her colour: white. She'd crossed over and, even without Dad, could never truly come back to her kind.

Barbara spent most of her life working in suburban Sydney, where she raised Debbie amongst Aboriginal people. There they were loved and accepted. Barbara never married, but her family has grown and she's now a proud matriach of an Aboriginal clan, living on a 'mission' in northern New South Wales. It was here I met her.

We talked easily over the next few days. I talked about Dad, and she talked about Dad. They were the same man, yet so very different. Mine had softened with age, his body now had no need of the muscles that he'd once worn as armour, and he held my children with a tenderness he would have once thought a sign of weakness. Barbara's man never had time to heal; he was buried in the hard, stony ground of the past. This was the early grave I'd always feared fate had dug for him; he was lying there with his dead daughter, my dead sister, Donna.

'You know about Donna? . . . Donna died when she was ten days old,' Barbara said.

I've always been touched by how old people can talk about dead children. At times it seems impersonal, almost macabre. I wonder if they seem real to them any more. Does time end when babies die? Because they haven't lived, do they somehow matter less? Or do they matter more . . . growing still inside their parents with a closeness that the living offspring will never enjoy?

'Do you know that song "Donna"?' Barbara asked me.

Yeah, I knew it. Dad had sung it often, an old song by Richie Valens. I thought it was just a pretty song.

'Your father used to sing that, when he'd play down the pub,' Barbara went on, enjoying this memory. 'I always said if you play that I'm leaving, but he'd sing it anyway.'

Now I remembered him singing it too: a sad song, a lament for a love lost.

'Do you want to see her photo?' Barbara asked. She didn't want an answer, she was already on her way to get it.

Now I had little baby Donna in my arms. My big sister. Oh, she was a beauty, Dad. So much life, and then so quickly gone. So much undone, so much unseen. All the possibilities of life . . . all of them and none. Yes, babies die, die all the time, needlessly, senselessly. But how much more painful, how much more senseless when the parents, too, are so young, and trying so hard and wanting something to believe in. I can't help thinking she died so that I would live, and if that's true, Dad, I hope she has the biggest room in your heart. She's lucky, Dad, that she had a big, strong father who'd carry her name in his hands and will one day be buried along with that name. And if the promise of heaven is worth anything, you will hold your little girl again.

I had no need of deep conversations with Debbie; they'd only embarrass both of us. The fact that we were together answered all our questions anyway. We laughed and went for walks. I played guitar. Debbie cooked for me, the kind of food my mum cooked when I was a boy: rabbit and roo in onion gravy with hot, fatty fried bread. It was just like our phone calls. When it was time to go we held each other close and cried.

'Thanks for coming,' she whispered. 'I'm not alone any more.'

She wasn't just talking for herself. I wasn't alone any more either . . . I'd met my father as well as my sister. I'd seen him at his best and his worst and I loved him more than ever.

2

Broken Biscuits Make You Cry

For Aboriginal people, resolving who is Aboriginal and who is not is an uneasy issue, located somewhere between the individual and the state.

MARCIA LANGTON, 'WELL, I HEARD IT ON THE RADIO AND I SAW IT ON THE TELEVISION' (1993)

I know love.

Love is going hungry so that others may be fed. It's little sacrifices that forsake a lifetime of joy so that others may know no pain. I know love because I know my mother.

I get my whiteness from my mother. I get my blackness from her too. Mum's blackness transcends colour; she can be as white as you think she is and yet as black as I know her to be. At once she conforms and confounds. The eugenic scientists of 1930s Australia would see in her pale face and narrow, pinched features the fufilment of their prophecy. Indeed, she is living proof of the fatal transience of Aboriginal blood. Here is a race that can be bred out, until none exist any longer.

Mum is black. She is black in ways whites do not understand, and she likes it like that. She doesn't have to explain; she doesn't have to apologise. You'd like me to explain here, I know. Australia is a remedial student of race; it's too easily confused. Where it fails to understand, it relies on the certainty of its law, the law that made this country legally white. Mum's white skin is a riddle to many — but not to her. She is more secure in her identity than any person I know. She's defied Australia's laws which have tried to tell her what she is. Mum is black; no need for me to explain, except to say that blood and love made her that way.

Blood and love. When she was asked to betray both she chose not to. My mother loved a black man. Not just a black man, but a wild black man. Somewhere she saw tenderness. She believed in him, and she had four children to prove it. She tamed my father by fighting him and caressing him, by throwing him out and taking him back. She tamed him by loving him.

'You bald, bony, rotten-toothed black mongrel!'

Yeah, that about said it. She said many things when they fought, and they fought often. One time she threw a tin of beans through the cupboard door, and complained only that she wasn't more accurate. She had no fear of him either . . . maybe she just trusted him. She punched him once when he wandered back home after going missing on a week-long drinking spree. One of the punches knocked him to his knees.

There were many times when I asked her to leave him. With a conceit worthy of Oedipus, I challenged my parents' love. Now, like Oedipus, I would stab out my eyes rather than see them apart. Theirs has been a love bigger than this country. I never really knew how big until Australia tried to say sorry. Three hundred thousand people walked across Sydney Harbour Bridge, but my eyes never left my mum and dad. They held hands and walked quietly with their memories, nothing left to know and no need to ask. I walked with them . . . offspring of their blood and their love.

When she was born, Betty Cameron had every right to believe she was white, every right to believe she was Australian. She was wrong. A blonde-haired, blue-eyed mother meant nothing when you had a broad-nosed, heavy-browed, white-skinned father. Yes, white-skinned. Mum's father was one of those amorphous characters whose appearance belies their race. A first glance would be deceptive, only the trained eye of a publican, a policeman or a welfare board officer could tell. But then, to Aborigines, who else mattered?

Mum was born in the 'good old days'. Life was simpler then. Before land rights or native title, before multiculturalism, refugees or reconciliation. Before Australia was confused by colour. In the 'good old days', Australia knew better. It knew well enough that Aborigines were better off locked on reserves lest they move into town. It knew well enough that Aboriginal children were often better off away from their parents. It knew well enough that Aborigines were better off without alcohol, that they were better off with someone else handling their money. It knew well enough that the police only had the blacks' best interests at heart. In this way Australia told itself — told us — that it cared.

My mother was born into a maze of legislation that defined us, then redefined us. When she was born the state could say she wasn't black at all. According to the *Aborigines Protection (Amendment) Act* 1936 the only Aborigines were 'Any full-blooded or half-caste aboriginal who is a native of Australia . . .' A light-skinned girl with a white mother and half-caste father clearly didn't qualify. Mum's mother, though, lived under threat of arrest for 'wandering with an Aborigine'. Mum's father was deemed too white to live on a reserve, yet too black to be accepted in town. His was a life lived on the fringes, where he was moved on at will by the police.

My grandfather, Keith Cameron, was born under a tree outside a little town called Baan Baa in northwest New South Wales. His mother was a Kamilaroi woman named Jessie Sutherland. His father could have been a half-caste or maybe a white man, no-one knows for sure. All we know is his name, Albert Cameron. My great-grandmother, Jessie, died giving birth, and her son survived with only one lung, leaving him constantly struggling to catch his breath. He was a proud man, a hard worker at whatever he could turn his hand to: gardening or the railway mostly. Despite his difficulty breathing, Keith showed a natural ability for tennis and even played professionally at Sydney's famed White City. He was known to everyone as Scales. I knew him as my pa. He lived with us, I loved him and he loved me.

'*Please release me, let . . .*'

Engelbert Humperdinck he wasn't.

'*For I don't love . . .*'

That's how we knew he was home. He'd rarely get the first verse out before he crashed into the side of the water tank or the outside toilet. Each pension day the routine was the same. He'd wait at our gate until the postman delivered his cheque, or his patience ran out. The postman could never get there quickly enough. Sometimes Pa would send me to track down the postie and fetch his cheque. Other times he'd march into the post office himself, especially if his cheque was late or, worse still, didn't arrive at all.

'Where's my money?' It was always *his* money, not the government's.

'Yeah, well it's all right for you, eh. Your white guts are full.'

Of course, filling his gut was the last thing on his mind . . . well, filling it with food anyway.

'If people don't like me they can just pass me by . . .'

He'd repeat that over and over as I helped him inside from wherever he'd fallen. Next morning I'd be up at dawn and on my hands and knees combing the grass for any coins that may have fallen out of my grandfather's pocket. I wouldn't keep any. He looked after me well enough; always made sure he bought me a bowl of ice cream and chocolate topping before heading for the pub. No, I'd keep his money for him or give it to Mum, who'd look after it until Pa was broke again.

One morning he woke to find all his money was gone.

'Have you bloody kids been into my pockets?' he yelled.

'No, Pa.'

He called for my mum.

'Betty . . . Betty! Someone's rolled me. I've lost all my money.'

'You couldn't have. Where were you last? Can you remember what you did?'

Yes, he could remember. He could remember going to the toilet before coming in. Our toilet was one of those old septic drums you'd find up the back yard. Each week it would fill up until the sanitary cart came around and emptied it. My grandfather struck a match and peered inside. His money was there all right, scrunched up and covered in the runny remains of last night's booze-up. Pa had mistaken his notes for toilet paper.

'Oh . . .' That's how Mum greeted any disaster. A shake of the head and an elongated sigh. It always ended with an upward inflection to emphasise whatever emotion was most appropriate. On this day it was disgust.

'Well, you've done it now,' she said.

She hadn't counted on Pa's attachment to his money. Slowly he rolled up his sleeve and plunged his hand into the drum. He had to lower his head halfway down the hole to reach, but neither sight nor smell would deter him. He didn't stop until he'd fished out every note, and then he went rummaging for the change. Carefully, he laundered his own cash, covered it in powder and hung the notes out on the line to dry. The publican would do a brisk trade again that night.

To put it crudely but truthfully, my grandfather had a close professional relationship with shit. At one time Pa used to drive the sanitary truck — 'the shit wagon', he called it. To Mum it may as well have been a Rolls Royce. Proudly she'd sit in the front seat and ask to be driven right up to the front gates of the school. Her father had a truck; that's what mattered, regardless of its contents. As he lived by human waste, so too did Pa almost die by it. He was mowing a woman's lawn for extra cash when he failed to notice an abandoned, but still fresh, sanitary pit. The boards covering the hole were not designed to withstand a seventeen-stone man. Pa was suddenly up to his armpits in the faecal bog and sinking fast.

'Oh well, I've lived in shit all my life and now I'm going to die in it.' That's all he could think of as he yelled to his cousin Neville to rescue him.

Neville Sutherland was half Pa's size, but that wasn't the biggest problem. Neville was three-parts deaf; what little hearing he had was drowned out by the lawnmower at the time. My grandfather could just about taste his fate when the woman who owned the house heard his distress call. Between them, she and Neville were able to winch Pa to safety.

I loved hearing these stories, and I'd sit with my grandfather for hours as he told them over and over. He was a master storyteller. They were always funny stories, but the humour came from lives where the only options were to laugh or cry. Aboriginal humour is like that; we're always telling jokes against ourselves.

'What's right and never fair?' Pa would ask. 'The left chin of a black gin!'

His family were especially funny. Pa told me about his cousin Bobby Cameron, who was so addicted to the television program 'Wyatt Earp' that it had ceased to be fantasy. Bobby would sit in front of the TV talking to the legendary US marshal; he'd even taken to keeping a gun by his chair in case Wyatt needed a hand. Once, when an outlaw was stalking his hero, Bobby yelled to Wyatt, 'Turn around! Turn around!' When Wyatt Earp failed to respond, his loyal deputy, Bobby, seized his rifle and fired wildly, dispatching his hero, the villain and the television set.

Then there was Pa's nephew, Owen. Owen was married once. 'Five years it lasted,' he said. 'Yeah, she didn't know I drank until I came home sober and she left me!' Owen lost not only a wife, but a great cook as well. 'She could cook two-minute noodles without even looking at her watch!' he said.

Mum's family lived for a time in an old house across from a church. One night the hall was being used for a celebration and the Good Samaritans thought they would send across the leftover food. My grandfather took one look at it and threw it out in disgust. 'What do they think we are . . . pigs or something?' he yelled. 'Look at this . . . they've even thrown their filthy wine slops in here.' The sweet delights of trifle were obviously wasted on a man more used to bread and jam.

These are the stories we like to remember. As I said, we laugh or we cry. My grandfather carried a sadness that he rarely let me see. It was a sadness of long-dead children, of love lost. They were his wounds, inflicted by a country that thought it had his best interests at heart. It was a sadness better off buried at the bottom of a bottle. It was a sadness he kept locked in his only worldly possession, a battered old brown suitcase he called his 'port'. Pa lugged that port from house to house as he made the rounds of his family. It held his clothes and his old cowboy comic books and a photo of a beautiful blonde woman he'd loved and would love until he died.

Ivy Sutton challenged and exposed white Australia's hypocrisy. She was a white woman who lived with a black man and had black kids. She didn't even bother with the niceties of marriage.

'I never married Pa,' she tells me now, 'because I never knew if I was going to leave him the next day.'

Life with my grandfather was the path of last resort for my nan. Her mother had kicked her out when she was a teenager and put her in a welfare home. The young Ivy tried to enrol at the local Catholic school in Coonabarabran. She was an inventive and precocious child who brushed up on her Christian studies to convince the nuns to take her.

'Where were you born?' they asked.

'Bethlehem,' she replied.

'Who are your parents?'

'Mary and Joseph.'

'Where were you baptised?'

'Down the River Jordan.'

Well, that was the end of that.

When Ivy finally got out of the girls' home, she knocked on her mother's door to be told her mum had remarried and her daughter still wasn't welcome. With nowhere to go, she remembered a young bloke who lived down by the river. He would whistle at her as she walked by. Keith was not only handsome, he had a tent! Ivy moved in that night and stayed more than twenty years, raising nine kids (and burying three more).

The law took a dim view of us then. Restrictive, oppressive legislation was designed supposedly for our welfare, but instead sucked the life out of black families. Amendments to the *Aborigines Protection Act* in 1936 gave magistrates the power to order blacks onto a reserve if they were living in poverty. It was a confusing twist on a law that was designed to drive more Aborigines off the reserves and into town. But the 'Dog Act', as it was known, was not for our benefit but to protect the sensitivities of whites who were offended by the sight of poor blacks on their streets. In 1939 the new *Child Welfare Act* gave the Aborigines Welfare Board the power to seize any Aboriginal child suspected of being neglected or uncontrollable. The pale faces of my mother and her brothers and sisters made them prime targets.

The welfare's in town!
The welfare's in town!
How fast the word gets around.

First they go to the schools,
to check the rolls and find
the fools who stay away;
'That just won't do,' we hear them say.
'Maybe we'll send the kids away.'

They go to our homes.
Don't knock, just walk in.
'Show me the clothes for
the children,' they'd say.
But there's not many clothes
when you don't get no pay.

'Where's the food?'
'What do they eat?'
'Show me the beds.'

'Where are the sheets?'
'We will report this, when the
Welfare Board meets . . .'

My mother's poems tell of the pain of those years. Of living one step ahead of the law. The welfare officers would march, uninvited, into my mum's family's house and search for signs of neglect. The first sight of the white government car would send black kids scattering, heading for the bushes. The fact that my grandmother was white did nothing to save her children. It counted against them: fair-skinned Aborigines were more easily absorbed into white society.

Tyranny was met with the blacks' ingenious resistance. They would collect as much food from each other as they could and stock their shelves. Flour would substitute for powdered milk, as they tried to fool the inspectors. As the welfare officers left by the front door, a runner would gather up all the tins and food and rush out the back into the next house. This scene would be repeated until the kidnappers had left.

My grandfather managed to keep his family together only by fleeing his home town. He'd been warned. His kids were next on the list. It wasn't an escape just from the welfare board, but also from the constant harassment of the police. My white nan was able to buy alcohol, and the police suspected she was running it onto the reserve. My grandfather was often arrested merely on suspicion of having been drunk. The police would come into his home and arrest him while he was in bed. Once they tied him to a tree and left him, like a dog, all day in the blazing sun. So he gathered his family and fled across the state to the little town of Stockinbingal. My nan's sister, Aunty May, lived there and told them it would be a safe place to hide out. They stayed there until it was safe to go home to Coona again.

Behind the law and the prying eyes and the deadly reach of welfare officers, a family tragedy had unfolded. Life was tough and cheap for Aboriginal families in the 1940s and 1950s. Death stalked the young and the old alike. My mum's brother, Kevin, remembers vividly the day the willy wagtail flew into their tin humpy. To my people the black and white bird is a harbinger of sorrow. My grandmother tried to chase it away, but it wouldn't leave. It sang its sad song and my nan knew her little boy was dead. The night before, my mum's little brother, Neville, had been rushed to the hospital with a high temperature. The policeman's knock at the door was a formality.

My grandparents, my mother, my uncles and aunties put tiny, ten-month-old Neville into a box, placed his little white booties and some wildflowers the kids had picked on top, and buried him in the ground.

My Uncle Kevin remembers that the police soon came again to my grandparents' home, this time with a gun and a bulldozer. My mother's family lived among a group of black families who'd built tin humpies on the outskirts of Coonabarabran at a place called Gunnedah

Hill. It was typical of the fringe settlements that had sprung up as more and more Aborigines either fled or were forced off the reserves. It was a precarious existence, dependent on the benevolence of the council or the patience of the local whites. Now time was up for Mum's family.

The land had been bought by a developer and one by one the blacks were run off. My grandfather had nowhere to go and was tired of running. He'd raised and buried his children here; this was his ancestors' land and he wouldn't budge. But the police were determined. As my grandmother cried and her children fled, the officer cocked his gun and aimed it at my grandfather's head. Pa dropped to his knees as the bulldozer ploughed into his little tin shack. Uncle Kevin has written about that day in a tiny unpublished journal he calls 'Looking Back'.

> It was like we were a part of our house too, and it was trying to help us somehow. But that big blade was too strong and the wire snapped and let go. Then our house came tumbling down and lay motionless in the dust. It was all over in a few seconds.

That night my mother, Uncle Kevin, their brothers and sisters and my grandparents slept under the stars.

Keith and Ivy didn't survive — couldn't survive — together. By the time Mum had me, my grandmother was married to another man and Pa was drifting from family to family. Their love was painful: the pain too great to sustain them, yet the love too deep to really keep them apart. They held each other in their hearts. Each year they'd run away together, recapturing their youth for a brief moment and glimpsing what might have been. Their holiday, they called it. But Nan would soon go back to her husband, Pa to his memories. Nan lived in a caravan at Narromine near her daughter Lorraine. Pa would often visit my aunty and sit at the window for hours, staring towards the river where his Ivy was camped.

'How much Aboriginal are you?'

It's a question my mother, and in turn her children, have been asked constantly. I've often struggled for an answer, my caramel skin and straight nose leaving me exposed and defenceless. Now the reply appears obvious: 'As Aboriginal as you've made me!'

White blood doesn't make you white. To imagine so renders us merely imitations of white people. To the whites of my mother's generation her pale skin was a mockery. She was too much like them, and they hated her for it. They hated her mother the most. Ivy Sutton ceased to be 'white'; she was 'black'. Black not by blood, but worse: by love. Being white never saved her children's lives. Being white didn't keep the welfare officers away. Being white didn't stop the police from destroying her home at the point of a gun.

Still, we reached out. As much as white Australia rejected us, we embraced them. My grandfather loved a white woman and never stopped loving her. For many of us, there is an inexorable drift to whiteness. Some have chosen to vanish altogether. They claim their white birthright by denying their black history. They live among you now, indistinguishable, often oblivious to their heritage. White Australia beckoned to my mother too. Her appearance offered a camouflage. Yet she chose a life with my father. She chose to embrace her blackness.

Mum and Dad began their married life in the shell of a broken-down Model T Ford on the Three-Ways Aboriginal reserve in Griffith. They pooled their pain and shared it evenly. They're in their sixties now and their battles have been fought and forgiven. My father's hands have held her world and Mum's the only person I know who's dried his tears. They're alone now with the snapshots of four decades of marriage. In their eyes I can see my father as a young man: pretty and dangerous. I see my mother: wiry and tough, with three children under three years old and spinning straw into gold. I see dusty roads and run-down sawmill shacks and rats so big they scrape the enamel off our dinner plates. I see hard work, hard years, and little change. I see courage and denial. I see my plate full and my mother's empty. I see my father's eyes: angry, hurt and mostly sad. And I see them now still loving each other, fear no longer outweighing hope.

My mother knows the pain of broken lives ... broken black lives. She knows enough of human frailty not to judge. She keeps her silences, and leaves others to theirs. And in her silence she remembers. She forgives, yes . . . but forgets, never. In her silence she's never far from Keith and Ivy, and her brothers and sisters and life on Gunnedah Hill.

Sometimes I picture through life's haze,
The humpy of my childhood days.
The dirt floors and the double bed,
Where five young children lay their heads.

Newspapers that lined the wall,
Keeping the chills from us all.
The cornbag quilts that kept us warm,
And the tanks that filled when we had a storm.

Kerosene lamps we used for light,
Candles when things were tight.
The ice-man that came around.
The path we used to take to town.

Speckled fruit Mum used to buy,
Rabbit we used to fry.
Broken biscuits made you cry,
I often think of days gone by.

BETTY GRANT, 'MY HUMPY HOME'

3

Canaan's Curse

For the State, a Nigger is a Nigger, is
A Nigger, sometimes Mr or Mrs or Dr Nigger.
JAMES BALDWIN, *THE EVIDENCE*
OF THINGS NOT SEEN

'I'm in the Lord's army . . . Yes, sir!'

'Jesus loves me, this I know, for the Bible tells me so . . .'

How I loved singing those songs at Sunday school. How I love to remember them now. There's a photo that goes with those songs: I'm with my sister, my hair slicked back in a wave, wearing a white shirt and black shorts, leaving home for church. The photo is blurry and tattered, but the clarity of my imagination compensates for my mother's lack of photographic acumen.

'I honour my God, I serve the Queen, I salute the flag . . .'

That daily school oath of allegiance also forms part of the bouquet of memories that sweetens the scent of my childhood. Together, they allow me to believe there was a time when race didn't matter.

'I'm in the Lord's army . . . YES, SIR!'

But there's another memory that sleeps in a darker corner of my mind. It taunts me, shames me. It's a hostile witness in my personal trial. It testifies against me, exposes my alibis and makes a liar of me. It leaves the jury of my conscience no choice but to find me guilty — guilty of not wanting to be black. My black alter ego saw my crime; my mother was my accomplice. She was the one who put enough white blood in my veins to tempt me. Mum was my example. She was at once black, yet white enough to pass unnoticed. It was as though she'd cracked the code of white society and I could too. All I needed — at least according to my self-hating five-year-old mind — was a cake of soap.

Mum stood at the bathroom door as I rubbed my skin red raw, rubbed my caramel skin 'white'. I don't recall what she said; in my memory she just smiles. I doubt she even remembers this; at her age she has enough memories of her own. But for me, this image defines me more than all the Sunday-school hymns and classroom pledges ever could. I was black — simple. I may as well have been an altogether separate species. There'd be as much chance of breeding a giraffe into a mouse as breeding me white. This was the prism of race, and I was trapped in it.

* * *

'What nationality are you?'

How many times have I been asked that question? How many conversations have been cut short by the answer?

'No, you couldn't be ...'

'But you don't ...'

'Really?'

Each question, each disbelieving stare, tempting me to deny the blood of my ancestors, to deny my parents.

How many times I've sat in the back of taxis, listening to the driver slander those 'bloody Abos', oblivious to my race. How many times I've sat there, shamed by my silence, preferring to endure the insult than reveal myself.

We've grown good at deceit, we pale-skinned, thin-lipped, straight-nosed half breeds. I have the perfect cover; my face asks more questions than it answers. A cursory glance in the mirror can't help but reveal the reflection of much of what passes, in the multicultural age, as generically 'Australian'. There's a bit of white, a hint somewhere of Chinese and, according to one of the names on my family tree (Naden), even some Afghan. Yet somehow these ancestral traces only go to form a kaleidoscope of Aboriginality, a human pinwheel of colours that can't help but merge into something the world can only identify as black. In the words of Shakespeare's Aaron the Moor, in *Titus*

Andronicus: 'For all the water in the ocean can never turn the swan's black legs to white.'

Even the lightest of us, the blond-haired, blue-eyed grandson of a full-blood counts himself among the sons of Ham, our biblical black progenitor, condemned by Noah to serve as the lowest of the low. The flotsam of the Ark washed up on antipodean shores as well, and I bear Canaan's curse today.

'You're not an Aborigine, you're a Maori.' My dear old Aunty May simply refused to accept the obvious. If we couldn't be white, then at least a more exotic, romantic form of black would do. Abos, as history told us often enough, were repugnant. We were condemned by the judgment of white men like explorer William Dampier, who turned his eyes from us as 'black, ugly and flyblown'.

Lighter skin was often a blessing — it allowed the conceit of superiority over our blacker cousins. Sometimes our delusion verged on comical. My youngest brother, Glen, once came home from school dishevelled and complaining of a sore head.

'What happened to you?' Mum asked.

'Oh, some blackies banged my head against a wall,' he said.

For a time we lived in a Housing Commission estate near a local black mission. Most of the assimilated blacks were moved there as a way of merging us into the community. We'd peer around the curtains, checking the main road in case any of those dangerous blackfellas might be walking past. Here we would pretend to be white; we were uptown, we rounded our vowels and paid special attention to pronouncing our aitches.

My mother would often shake her head when she heard us talking in the pidgin slang of our kin. 'If you don't stop that, you'll talk like that forever,' she'd say.

To my parents the whiter we could act, the easier our future would be. Who could blame them? They'd endured lifetimes of torment and violence, and all I needed to do was look around to see there was little joy in being black. The whites may have despised us, but we reserved a special venom for each other. There was scant unity in our blackness — we stole from each other, we slept with each other's wives and husbands, we lied to each other and we bashed each other. My father told me of one brawl at a wedding on the mission, where his uncle grabbed another man and dragged him along a barbed-wire fence and tore out half his back. Dad threw off his jacket to join in; when the fighting was over, he found that his wallet had been stolen.

Violence became a test of manhood, our worth measured by how much damage we could inflict. Men fought at home, in pubs, along the railway track or banks of the irrigation channel. Legends were made of men who'd had the skin stripped from their faces yet come back again for more. The savagery was repulsive and irresistible at the same time. Brutality was somehow noble; these men, heroes. Our elders no longer carried the scars of ritual but of drunken battle. My father had won the status of a hard man.

When I was thirteen, I saw another warrior made before my eyes.

All day the young black men of our town had gathered outside the grog tent at the annual agricultural show. This was a time-honoured clearing house of aggression, as scores were settled here. Their fathers had come here, and their fathers before them. Some walked away men; most were sacrificed to the myth that would be told and re-told, as I'm doing now.

The grog made the timid brave, and the sun beat down that day, slowly bringing meanness to the boil. What started the fight hardly matters; what I do know is how it finished. I can still recall the sickening thuds as my cousin Fred's fists sunk deeper and deeper into his hapless victim's gut. Never did Fred's blows move to the head. He carefully aimed under the rib cage, each blow delivered with the ferocity of a pile driver. He didn't stop until he'd stolen the other man's pride.

Don't give me the Dreamtime. This is where Aboriginal identity was forged where I came from. Some women even measured love by the number of bruises on their bodies. I didn't grow up with dot paintings and corroborees; ours was a world of broken glass and mangy dogs. For a long time we tried to avoid other blacks, preferring the ignominy of fringe dwellers, clinging to the promise of the white in us. Then we'd rub against our black reality once again and cringe against our fate. There was nothing here that spoke to me of pride or even survival. There was nothing here to put on a tourist brochure.

* * *

I'd like to say I grew out of wanting to wash myself white. Maybe I could invent a life in which I stood up for myself and fought against injustice, but that would be a lie. No, my childhood snapshots are of running away, shrinking from and making excuses for being an Aborigine. I recall when my best friend, Owen Flottman, and I ran home to his mother in tears because kids at school had teased us for being black. In Owen's case it was doubly confusing, because his mum and dad were white. Mr Flottman was the local Presbyterian minister and he and his wife had adopted half a dozen Aboriginal children. Dear Mrs Flottman couldn't bring herself to say the word 'black'. Instead she put one of her big arms around us and told us to be proud of our 'lovely olive skin'. Trouble was, we weren't proud of it; if we were, we wouldn't have been so upset.

Yet despite our denials, our delusion or shame, in the eyes of whites we were only ever blacks. My childhood was spent on the road. My family moved around so much I was rarely at one school long enough for anyone to notice anything about me save the fact I was black. Never mind that I wasn't so much darker than a lot of them; I was dark enough for them to notice. I never heard anyone call me a 'part-Abo'; I was always 'that new black kid'. It didn't help either that we were dirt poor — strike two against me.

I added it up once: I started at a dozen new schools before I was twelve. Sometimes we'd land in a town with a lot of other blacks, and then I'd have someone to fight my battles for me. I remember a boy called Freeman in Tumut, and a blind alley with me on the run and half a dozen white boys in pursuit. I would have been no more than ten years old and scared out of my wits when my black saviour came to my aid and turned the white posse on its heels.

Griffith was the place where I felt most at home — the place where I was born. When we lived in Griffith there was safety in numbers; there were people who looked like me. Griffith High School was split three ways: the Italian kids stuck together, the white kids stuck together and the Aborigines stuck together. In the pragmatic world of schoolboy racial politics we would sometimes sit with the Italians, but not the whites. When we'd play football it'd be blacks versus whites, and if we were short a player we'd grab one of our swarthy dago mates. We terrorised the schoolyard, winning back some of the respect and power we were denied outside it. Even racial stereotypes worked in our favour: all blacks can fight, so stay away from the blacks.

But reputation only lasts so long; every once in a while someone has to get hit to maintain the order. This time it was my turn. Brett Ole was a white kid who liked to hang around us, and we liked him up to a point. A couple of black kids decided that point had been reached. I was the one who would have to teach him a lesson, remind him he was just a 'gubbah' — a whitey.

A dangerous man is someone who doesn't know who he is or where he belongs. Good sense gives way to the pressing need for approval, and the older Aboriginal boys were goading me where I was most vulnerable, challenging my fragile black pride. As I cornered Brett Ole in the cloakroom, I wasn't fighting him, I was fighting myself. My father had taught me not to waste time talking in a fight, not to grab collars, to keep both hands free and open up with all guns blazing. I followed his instructions to the letter. I was bigger than Brett and pounded him into a corner, where I continued to flail away at his face until it turned blue and my hands ached. Abruptly, I stopped — this was sick. As I walked away Brett swung a round-arm king-hit into my lip; it split open and poured blood. I just kept walking, perversely glad he'd evened the score.

This was a glimpse of a parallel universe in which violence became a habit, a lifestyle even. Nothing separated me from my friends and cousins for whom such a fate appeared preordained — nothing but fate itself. Within months my family moved again, this time to Canberra. But not before the principal at Griffith High told me he didn't want me there anyway; in fact it appeared to me that he didn't want any Aboriginal boys once we'd reached the age of fifteen. Education, he said, would be wasted on us, and too many of my mates believed him.

It's a funny thing, but in Griffith I was an 'Abo'; in the city I was suddenly an 'Aborigine' or, better still, an 'Aboriginal'. What a difference a word can make. Replacing the noun with an adjective somehow made what I was less offensive, less threatening; it made it easier for white people to say. If you couldn't be white then the next best thing was to be an Aboriginal. Abos we know only as statistics: they drink too much; they steal; they bash and rape; they get locked up; they hang themselves in jail. Abos scare whites; Aboriginals make them feel sorry. Aboriginals let whites believe in the Australian egalitarian myth, believe in a 'fair go'; Abos remind whites it's a lie. You can see an Abo in any Australian country town: they have a hardness about them, a sense of danger; they keep their eyes down; to white eyes they're shiftless and untrustworthy. Aboriginals are harder to spot: they live next to you; send their kids to your schools; you might bump into them in the supermarket — you wouldn't even know. Aboriginals could be Greeks or Italians maybe; if pushed, Indians or Maoris. I was an Abo when I bashed Brett Ole; in Canberra I was an Aborigine well on the way to being an Aboriginal.

If the black man wants to keep dying in Australia, all he needs to be is an Abo. Abos are not born, they're made. Abos are Australia's afterbirth, the mess whites have so far failed to clean up. Abos are lost causes. Abos don't exist in the popular imagination without adjectives: the 'lazy Abo', the 'ungrateful Abo' or the 'drunken Abo'. Aboriginal anthropologist Professor Marcia Langton says such terms lock blacks into a prison of neglect:

> Today it remains the background and popular explanation for the extraordinary arrest rates of Aboriginal people, for the continuing exclusion of Aboriginal people from employment, education, health services and rental accommodation.

Of course, as we know, as a thousand radio talkback callers will tell you: 'Abos get too much.'

Australia gave up on Abos in the 1930s; so, too, if we're honest, did the aspiring Aboriginals. James Baldwin once wrote that in America 'nothing is as important as being white'. Australia is no different, yet I wonder if Aborigines don't value it even more. In the 1930s a new policy offered so many blacks a way out. No humiliation would be too much to bear, no betrayal too great, to help fulfil Australia's 'final solution' of assimilation. The promise of 'absorption into the Commonwealth of Australia' was a clarion call for barely black people who felt that was where they belonged anyway.

Aboriginal reserves became training grounds where blacks could be taught how to be white. For those who made the grade there was the promise of town housing, the opportunity to sip tea with white neighbours. Some blacks could even apply for exemption certificates — or 'dog tags' — which meant they became honorary whites, able to claim social services benefits and even purchase alcohol. First, though, they had to prove they were civilised; they had to abandon those heathen tribal ways. Reserve managers were known to chastise Aborigines for wailing at funerals, saying it impeded assimilation. Aboriginal grandparents refused to speak their languages, and ended the traditional ceremonies of initiation.

So the mission blacks became 'respectable'. They boasted of keeping their dirt-floor humpies spotlessly clean, they wore collars and ties and went to church on Sunday. But they weren't free and they weren't accepted. If they went to the cinema they sat in a section roped off from whites; they were still barred from clubs and pubs. Yet they convinced themselves they were white in all but skin colour, and even that could be fixed in one generation with a white son- or daughter-in-law. Segregation and prejudice made intermarriage difficult, but not impossible. Among blacks a white spouse was a status symbol. Dr Ruth Fink surveyed the people of Brewarrina in 1957 and found that among twenty-five Aboriginal families who thought themselves superior to other blacks, in almost half the cases their claim to status was being married to a white person.

In less than two hundred years whites had successfully dispossessed Aborigines, rendered them powerless in their own land, in some cases massacred them and then tried to legislate them out of existence. Yet their greatest success was in convincing blacks to be like them. We wanted to be citizens, we wanted to vote, we fought in their wars and even tried to love them. Survival pays no reward for loyalty. Full-bloods, darker-skinned Aborigines and those simply deemed unworthy of 'civilising' were left behind to rot on derelict reserves. In New South Wales the Aborigines Protection Board stopped repairing the already dilapidated houses; they swooped on children they claimed were in danger and watched the slow death of a generation.

These are the Abos, left not with pride but resentment. They don't like white people, they don't trust them, they use them more than tolerate them. They guard themselves with an impenetrable squalor; they call the government's bluff and they mock the efforts of the Aboriginals. Abos have names for their upwardly mobile cousins: 'uptown blacks', 'coconuts' — brown on the outside, white on the inside — and 'gubbahrigines', based on their slang term for white people. The Aboriginals don't escape either — they bequeath to their descendants a legacy of betrayal and lingering shame.

I've lived my life caught between the promise of whiteness and the reality — all too often, brutal reality — of my blackness.

As a child, I often hoped no-one would notice my blackness, and when they did my hesitation would deny two thousand generations of my ancestors. There were times when I tried to hide my father from my white friends, ashamed of what he represented. Each step I took was another step closer to becoming white, until eventually I became a success. Success for a black person can be the white man's cruellest trick; it allows us to grow complacent, comfortable, respectable. Eventually, so we are told, we even become role models.

Where do I get the conceit to excuse driving my new BMW into the black ghetto of Sydney's Redfern to talk to my black 'brothers and sisters'? How can I look them in the eye and dare to claim them as my people? If Aborigines are poor, I'm not an Aborigine; if Aborigines are coal black, I'm not an Aborigine; if Aborigines are the victims of injustice and bigotry, I'm not an Aborigine.

To millions of Australians I am just a face on television. I exist in a sort of cultural void, a colourless, raceless twilight zone, where my life ceases to have real meaning outside the black box in the corner of the living room. What did my race matter, when all that was asked of me was that I appear in the corner of people's living rooms each night?

From behind the studio desk I looked out into the homes of people who may not have been so welcoming had I not entered under the guise of celebrity. Others, though, congratulated themselves that Australia had broken through the colour barrier, that in me they had the first Aboriginal news or current affairs presenter on commercial TV. My executive producer, Gerald Stone, was an American and familiar with black people on television, and he saw my role as a great step forward. He supported me, and still does. Yet I felt my being an Aborigine also became a gimmick, another tool for television promotion.

Television scribes mined the cliché 'poor black boy makes good'. I made the rounds of Aboriginal organisations, schools and prisons as living proof that we can make it in the white world. My example, though, was in the futility of community life and the salvation of selfish individualism. I could have been a poster boy for assimilation, and that other blacks lauded me for it only revealed their barely hidden aspirations.

The price of success for someone who likes to call himself an Aborigine is conformity. He is expected to play by the rules, both white and black. The white story is that Australians are a tolerant people, committed to a fair go for all; the black story is that we are the proud standard-bearers of the oldest, most peaceful and spiritually transcendent culture on Earth. These are Australia's romantic myths and I am their synthesis, just like all the emerging and successful black actors, dancers, artists and sportspeople.

White Australia historically has had no tolerance for Aborigines. Instead it has tried to remake us in its image. It has bought, bribed or beaten us into submission. It has flattered us and courted us. The dividing line has become so blurred that we no longer know where it is. Aboriginality has grown more malleable as the bloodlines have become increasingly tenuous. Nouveau Aborigines now see it as somehow chic. For some it has become a kind of cultural curio, a dark secret to be unearthed from their family's past and fashioned into a new identity. For these people it's a way of atoning for their family's lies and shame.

Only they knew the times they crossed the street to avoid the inquiring eyes of the blacks; how they anxiously studied the faces of their children, hoping they didn't betray the telltale features of their hidden ancestry, and only they know the lies they told those same children if they did.

For all the ingredients of contradiction, confusion and downright forgery that make up Aboriginal identity, still I yearn for my blackness. It's still where I find meaning. In the company of my kin I can truly feel at home. In them I find kindness, laughter and dignity. Where as a child I sought distance, now I seek shelter. Being an Aborigine is often the only thing that truly makes sense of my world. Yes, it's confusing, but why wouldn't we be confused living in a country that has often told us what we are not, then made us realise we could be no other.

I look out on the world through the eyes of my ancestors, and if whites get too close they also see the reflection of something they thought — they hoped — they'd destroyed. When I finally left Channel 7, one of the managers there asked me, 'Why don't you go back to your tribe?' But where is my tribe? Who is my tribe? Author Sally Morgan, who has struggled with her own family's black identity, says we meet ourselves in the past. I know I am the son of Stan Grant, who is the son of Cecil Grant, the son of Bill Grant, the son of a man unknown. Who I am remains trapped in time and tragedy and love and hope and, somewhere, freedom.

4

Man of Fire

. . . as time went on the colour of the blacks seemed to grow paler and paler, until at last only the white faces of the Wundah (spirits of the dead) and white devils were to be seen, as if it should mean that some day no more blacks should be on this earth.

MRS LANGLOW PARKER,
THE EUAHLAYI TRIBE

The whites called him Windradyne; some simply knew him as Saturday. To his people he was Wiindhuraydhine; his name meant 'having fire'. For three bloody years, between 1822 and 1825, the great Wiradjuri leader fought the British in a battle for his land and the freedom of his people. So brutal was the conflict that Governor Brisbane declared martial law, setting in place a legal war of extermination.

This is where Australia began the big lie. This is where white settlers hunted my ancestors down like dogs, and then told us it never happened. War? To call it a war would at least accord us the respect of the vanquished; we're not even worthy of that. There was no war in Australia, not in my schoolboy history books. Australians fought bravely on the battlefields of Europe; blood never stained the wattle. The blacks were timid, passive; they simply faded from the frontier.

The whites, as an ancient Roman once said, made their solitude and called it peace. As a boy there was no pride to be found in the deeds of cowardly, dim-witted blacks; the only heroes of Australia were white. I loudly cheered for my school sports house, Lawson, not knowing its namesake, William Lawson, the conqueror of the Blue Mountains, had conspired to round up and kill my people. No teacher told me that he helped drive hundreds of Aboriginal women and children to their deaths. No-one told me about Wiindhuraydhine.

'If this was America, he'd be as well known as Geronimo,' John Suttor says.

The ageing white farmer has a bond with Wiindhuraydhine, forged in blood. The old black warrior rests amidst the sloping hills of Suttor's family property, Brucedale. John Suttor is a wiry old man who greets me with a firm grip and a clear eye. He's spent a lifetime here; he's defined by this land as much as any of the people who claim the blood of the Wiradjuri. John Suttor has a glorious traitor's heart; at least, he's a traitor to patriots who substitute folklore for fact. His treachery, though, is naive, an honesty that allows him to speak simple truths. The truth for Suttor is not to be weighed and measured, distorted for political or moral gain. This makes him rare and dangerous.

John Suttor is 'comfortable and relaxed' about history, but not, I suspect, in the way the prime minister, John Howard, conceives of the phrase. Suttor has no need of Howard's white blindfold and I doubt whether he's a champion of black orthodoxy, which can concede no failing or ill-doing of its own. Perhaps he puts no store in apologies or reconciliation, land rights or the so-called 'stolen generation'. Perhaps; I didn't bother to ask. I know only that there is a wonderful symmetry in my coming here, in learning of my past from a man who has no allegiance other than to the land that sustains him, a man I can trust to 'give it to me straight'.

'There were great atrocities committed on all sides,' John says to me.

'Do many people come here now?' I ask.

'No, not any more. There used to be a few, but he's been pretty much forgotten,' he says.

Wiindhuraydhine lies below a grassy mound. The area is fenced off and another of the Wiradjuri dead rests in a similar grave nearby. The cemetery is marked by a plaque which reads:

> *The resting place of Windradyne, alias Saturday, the last chief of the Aborigines.*
> *First a terror, but later a friend to the settlers. Died of wounds received in a tribal encounter 1835.*
> *A true patriot.*

In the crisp air of autumn, the landscape softened by the golden tips of the trees, I'm with the spirits of my ancestors. As a chill breeze whispers through the valley, it carries the story of what happened here. Of how Wiindhuraydhine raised himself to repel the invaders — the men he called the Wandang, the white ghosts whose evil magic had killed so many of his people.

There's a stillness here that could easily be called serenity, but it's not. It's a far more sinister silence — the silence of the dead. The land caresses the wail of its people, gently quietening them with the promise that the wind won't forget them, that it will carry the echo of their cry for eternity. The rocks, the trees, the hills are nature's sentinels, guarding the past until we're old enough to gaze on it with humility, until we no longer feel compelled to plunder it for gain. This land terrifies Australians. I'd never known how great the fear was until I drove here for the first time, with my eyes truly opened.

I crossed the Blue Mountains on a road that runs not far from where Blaxland, Lawson and Wentworth first trekked. Houses cluster together in villages where people convince themselves they're getting away from it all, living closer to nature. The truth is they're like children who can't sleep without the light on; they cling to the roadside for reassurance that there is a way out. It points them in the direction of the sea and ultimately to their real homes — the distant ports from which their forebears first set sail. They don't live in this country; they're just camping out.

To placate their fears, Australians make up poems about loving a sunburnt country, a land of sweeping plains, of rugged mountain ranges, of droughts and flooding rains. All the while they huddle against it, living cheek to jowl along narrow strips of coast, cringing against the vast, unknowable expanse of the interior they call the outback. Dorothea Mackellar did not compose an ode, but a warning; a warning about beauty and *terror*. People vanish out there, lured by sirens, never to return. Explorers perished; they died of thirst and hunger and Australians still have not gone looking for them.

The outback holds a macabre fascination: babies with darkly suggestive names are taken by dingoes, and tourists are waylaid by wandering killers who, with their prey, dissolve back into the darkness whence they came. A crime that would occur every day in the city takes on a more sinister form if it happens out there. This is a place of death, and Australians are afraid of ghosts.

Australians don't go outback, not just because they might die, but because they might kill. For here is another side to the story of this nation: not a fairytale about lovably roguish convicts or brave pioneers, but a more confronting tale of murder. Here there is no distraction, just a relentless, throbbing silence, and a murmur of foul deeds. Out here black babies had their heads caved in with rocks; women were raped and filled with disease then shot where they lay; men were castrated and decapitated, their heads pickled and displayed in museums. No conscience can withstand that, so we choose to avoid it. In the words of historian Bernard Smith, Australia is plagued by guilt.

John Suttor, though, has made his peace here. He's better than me: I'm afraid, or worse, ashamed. John's family's ghosts walk with mine, and he does our job for us, tending them, black and white alike.

'Just over there, that old hut, that's where Windradyne confronted my great-grandfather,' John says.

The hut is now a shell. But on that night of 23 May 1824 it played a part in one of the great battles of Bathurst. John Suttor keeps a copy of a book by his great-uncle, William Henry Suttor. It's called *Australian Stories Retold*, an ironic title because these stories were never told in the first place. As I thumb its pages, I'm torn in two. I wonder: how do I stand here today with the blood of the killer and killed in my veins? How can one part of me do that to the other?

> The blacks were troublesome at Bathurst in those days, the cause very frequently was their ill-treatment by the whites. No wonder reprisals took place. Our

> hut was one day surrounded by a large party of blacks, fully equipped for war, under the leadership of their great fierce chief and warrior, named by the whites Saturday. There was no means of resistance so my father, then a lad of eighteen years, met them fearlessly at the door.

So wrote William Henry Suttor. His father, William Suttor senior, was one of the first white men to gaze upon this land. He staked the claim that is the home today of his great-grandson, John. It's nestled in a rolling valley, dotted with eerie rock formations that mark not just the land but the slow passage of time. Some are like history books, carrying the crude markings that my ancestors used to explain their place in the universe. John believes they were once important ritual sites for the Wiradjuri. He respects this place, as old William respected the people who brought him here. If it wasn't for the blacks, the Suttor family would not be living here today.

'He was supposed to take up land where the Macquarie River runs north of the township,' John says. 'Well of course the river runs west, so the blacks told Great-grandfather about this land where the two creeks meet and this is where he settled.'

William Suttor knew this land did not speak English; to talk to it he must learn the sounds of the Wiradjuri. As he met Wiindhuraydhine that night, it's what saved his life. His son described the tense standoff:

> He spoke to them in their own language in such a manner as not to let them suppose he anticipated any evil from them. They stood there, sullen, silent, motionless. My father's cheerful courage and friendly tone disarmed animosity. They consulted in an undertone and departed as suddenly, noiselessly, as they came.

Suttor was spared but the warriors were intent on bloodshed. Within twenty-four hours Wiindhuraydhine launched a raid on a property then known as Millah-Murrah. Today it is remembered chillingly as Murdering Hut. The property was owned by Samuel Terry, a man described by Bathurst historian P.J. Gresser as a 'dubious character'. It's believed Terry had built his homestead on a Bora ground. This was a place sacred to the Wiradjuri, the site of initiation ceremonies where young boys were turned into men. Revenge was on the warriors' minds. By the time the raid was finished, three station hands were dead and everything that had been built on the sacred site was destroyed. The 'murdering hut' itself is gone, but if you go to the site today, in the right light you can see still the outline of the old Bora ground.

History belongs to the white man; it is a white story. As James Baldwin wrote, history is a hymn to white people, and all of us others have been discovered. Whites only allow us to enter their history on their terms. So it is that I tell this story not from the memory of my own people, the defeated, but from the records of the victors. I'm left to piece together the second-hand accounts of what may or may not have happened here, but dates, times, places, numbers matter less than the damage they've inflicted on our psyche. I need to come here to understand where my family's story truly begins — not in the hazy mythology of the Dreamtime, but in the very red brutality of the Australian frontier.

As I devour the public records, I'm erasing the shame of the child who was brainwashed into believing his people fled without honour. It's a perverse pride: one gained from murder. Yet, am I any different to white Australians? You nourish a nation on the vainglorious tale of a bungled invasion of a beach in Turkey. Wiindhuraydhine is a hero I need, just as you need Simpson and his donkey. It's a shame we all don't know more of him, for then maybe you could honour him too on your memorials.

Once, Australians did know of him, and they followed his barbarous rampage with fear. The *Sydney Gazette* reported the running battles almost daily. On 10 June 1824, it told of an attack on a property known as Warren Gunyah, near Wattle Flat. It was owned by a man named Tindell and three of his men were slaughtered.

> Three other unfortunate fellow creatures, servants to Mr Tindell, also fell victims to the barbarity of these mountaineers; two of them having been burnt to death in the hut; and the other had no less than five spears through the body, and one through each hand.

Warren Gunyah, like Millah-Murrah, was stripped bare, every building ransacked. The war party moved on to a place known as the Mill Post. A hut was stripped and the hutkeeper killed. A survivor wrote to the Reverend W.M. Horton and told of the atrocities at the three stations:

> Thus seven poor men all lost their lives in one day; it was truly shocking to see them. Each of them that were in the hut had one leg burnt off and the other terribly mangled by the tomahawks — I was very near experiencing the same fate myself — had I been feeding my sheep in any other direction than where I was I could not have escaped, but thanks be to God that he directed my steps out of the way.

Wiindhuraydhine had lit the fuse for an explosion of violence throughout the district. By the end of May other blacks had taken up arms. At one property on the O'Connell plains, an overseer reported seeing fifty armed warriors. Huts were raided and stock killed or turned loose. Finally William Lane, the overseer on a property owned by Samuel Hassall, armed six of his servants and set off in revenge. The vigilante party came upon a group of about thirty Wiradjuri people and opened fire. Three women were killed in the attack and their bodies thrown into a waterhole. The *Sydney Gazette* on 10 June expressed outrage at the atrocity: 'Heaven will not readily absterge so foul a stain — how then is it to be expected that man should justify such bloodstained guilt.'

In one month at least thirteen white men had been killed. An unknown number of blacks were massacred in reprisals; some reports of the day put it as high as seventy. Outrage grew among the community as pressure built on the authorities to stem the bloodshed. The solution was not conciliation; the whites had come to the Wiradjuri land, and they'd come to stay. As P.J. Gresser would later write in his historical sketch *The Aborigines of the Bathurst District*, 'the story of European settlement in the Bathurst district is also the story of Aboriginal decimation, decay and death'. A letter to the editor in the *Sydney Gazette* on 12 August summed up the local mood:

> Every true friend of the Aborigines must desire that they should be made to learn by terror those lessons which they have refused to acquire under a milder discipline. We are now to oppose strength to strength, that an end may be put to the effusion of human blood.

Two days later Governor Brisbane declared martial law with the words:

> Mutual bloodshed may be stopped by the use of arms against the Natives beyond the ordinary Rule of Law in Time of Peace; and for this end, resort to summary Justice has become necessary . . .

'Beyond the ordinary Rule of Law in Time of Peace . . .' The proclamation made it clear that the time of peace had ended; a time of war had begun. By October the *Sydney Gazette* was describing the situation around Bathurst as an exterminating war. For the first and only time on Australian soil the slaughter of my people — the Wiradjuri — was legally sanctioned. To enforce the declaration, the local military was bolstered with reinforcements. John Suttor's great-uncle, William Henry Suttor, wrote of the horrifying impact of martial law:

> Under this condition of things the blacks were shot down without any respect. Getting the worst of it, most of them made out into the deep dells of the Capertee country and although some escaped, many were killed there.

In Suttor's mind the proclamation of martial law was as indecipherable to the Wiradjuri as an Egyptian hieroglyph. His book includes one account of an attack so callous, it can't help but leave the reader numb. A party of soldiers was sent to deal with a camp of blacks.

> Negotiations, apparently friendly, but really treacherous, were entered into. Food was prepared, and was placed on the ground within musket range of the station buildings. The blacks were invited to come for it. Unsuspectingly, they did come,

> principally women and children. As they gathered up the white men's presents they were shot down by a brutal volley, without regard to age or sex.

To my people the great evil had come to their land and death seemed their only fate; those who were left lived in a world no longer of their making. The explorer Sir Thomas Mitchell wrote of the blacks having no comprehension of the weapons of the whites. They looked upon the guns as magic sticks more powerful than their own death-dealing pointing-bones. The dreaded white ghosts' magic sticks were pointed at the Wiradjuri, and Wiindhuraydhine was their prime target. The commandant at Bathurst, James Thomas Morisset, had declared the warrior chief as the district's greatest enemy, issuing a notice through the Colonial Secretary's office:

> FIVE HUNDRED ACRES OF LAND to be
> given to any Person who will bring in Saturday,
> alive, to any magistrate of the territory.
> By His Excellency's Command,
> F. Goulburn, Colonial Secretary

How different it had been less than ten years earlier when Wiindhuraydhine had met with another white chief, Governor Lachlan Macquarie. Then they'd met in peace, and the governor had left with the promise that the Wiradjuri would come to no harm. What had happened?

The fate of the Wiradjuri, the fate of all the people of this land, was sealed on an April day in 1770 at what is now known as Botany Bay. Seeing the English ship *Endeavour* anchor in the bay, two Gamaraigal men mounted the first act of resistance. Watching thirty or forty men approach in rowing boats, the warriors stood on the shore with their woomeras and spears. They'd seen nothing like this before: the pale colour of these men, their bodies fully covered in cloth; their boats, and their weapons. It took only minutes before they felt the full power of the gun.

As the men stood their ground an English officer ordered a shot be fired over their heads. The sound forced the younger man to drop his weapons, but bravely he picked them up again and gestured to the newcomers to retreat. The next shots were not aimed above their heads and the older man was wounded. The very act of claiming this land for Britain had come at the cost of Aboriginal blood. As historian Geoffrey Blainey says in his book *Triumph of the Nomads*: 'the civilisation of iron and gunpowder was confronted by the flimsy weapons of wood and bone.'

It would be another forty-three years before the Wiradjuri would see whites. There's little doubt, however, that the people west of the Blue Mountains would have been expecting them. Before the whites came, the people of this land communicated and traded with each other across vast distances. Blainey tells of stone axes, mined and shaped near Melbourne, being used to cut wooden canoes along the Murray, more than

300 kilometres away. I can imagine Wiindhuraydhine growing into a man and hearing the legend of the white sails which brought the strange men to his neighbours' country. Perhaps he was emboldened by the stories of Mosquito and Pemulwuy, who'd led the war of resistance as the penal colony of New South Wales stretched out to the hills. Pemulwuy was eventually shot, his head severed and pickled and sent as a gift to Sir Joseph Banks in England.

It was on the evening of 21 December 1813 that certainty ended for the Wiradjuri and the fate of my family was sealed. I know only as much of that world, that time, as anthropologists have told me. I know our society was basic: our small population posed no questions of democracy or revolution; we built no great monuments to ourselves, or cities; we'd not discovered the life-altering potential of the wheel. We were in no way prepared for the onslaught of a people whose transport and weapons put them centuries ahead of us. What sophistication we had was in our spirituality, born of a relationship with a land that is more prone to destroy than nurture.

Some Aborigines comfort themselves with a belief in a tribal utopia, devoid of war, famine or disease. They like to imagine themselves as *homo naturalis*, with no need for guile or cunning, no appetite for deception. Others imagine a world of greater political acuity; they eschew the word 'tribe' for the more grand epithet of 'nation'. In the absence of any traditional knowledge they appropriate European terms like ‘confederation’ to describe what was a loose affiliation of clans.

In reality, two hundred years ago there was no parliament for us to convene, no diplomats for us to dispatch to broker a deal with the whites; we met them not with knowledge but with superstition.

I like to think it was a hot evening, one of those oppressive nights I remember from my childhood, with heatwaves shimmering in the air and nostrils burning from the swirling seeds of the long dry grass. In the stillness a soft breeze rustles through the trees bringing the promise of the cool relief of night. On that December evening George William Evans stooped to drink from the river where he and his party of five men had made their camp. Evans, the colony’s Deputy Surveyor General, was on a mission to explore the vast expanse west of the Great Dividing Range. Only six months earlier Gregory Blaxland, William Charles Wentworth and William Lawson had conquered the Blue Mountains that had stood as a jailer locking the burgeoning colony on the coastline. The successful crossing meant Macquarie was free to pursue his dream of a nation built on the sweat of emancipated convicts. Evans ran his eye over the fertile hills and plains that surrounded him and knew that he’d found the land the governor desired.

George Evans cast his net to fish in the river he’d named the Macquarie, but he was puzzled. In the month since he and his party had set out on their journey he’d felt he’d been watched. Who made the fresh tracks he followed? Who lit the still-smouldering camp fires he stumbled upon? Just two weeks earlier, on 6 December 1813, he'd written in his diary: 'I conceive it strange we have not fell in with natives. I think they are watching us, but are afraid.'

He would not have to wonder any more. Suddenly there was a gut-wrenching howl and Evans looked up to see two women and four children who'd come to the river for water. To the Wiradjuri this was the Wombool, the great river that had sustained the people for an eternity. Now, it seemed it gave life to new people. Evans witnessed a scene of utter fear, and in his summary of his journey wrote:

> The most remarkable occurrence during my journey was my suddenly coming upon two native women and four children, whose terror and surprise exceeded all belief. Violently trembling, they fell down before me, and it was some time before they would venture to look up.

Evans calmed the women's fear and offered them a tomahawk and fish-hooks. They ran away, never looking back. As Evans returned over the mountains he was followed by smoke from the camp fires of the Wiradjuri people. Historian P.J. Gresser speculated that the columns of smoke may have been signals to warn groups ahead that the strangers were coming.

Evans spoke so glowingly of the land he'd seen that Governor Macquarie ordered a road be built over the mountains to open up the interior. On 4 May 1815 Macquarie himself arrived in the region and in his journal described his first encounter with the blacks:

> They were all clothed with mantles made of opossum skins, which were very neatly sewn together. The outside of the skins were carved in a remarkable neat manner. They appear to be very inoffensive and cleanly in their persons.

Macquarie had been grappling with the stubborn black resistance from the natives around Sydney. In 1816 he would forbid Aborigines to carry weapons within two miles of a house or town. Concerned at the escalating violence, he gave settlers permission to establish vigilante groups and ordered that the ten most wanted Aboriginal 'murderers' were to be shot on sight.

As a man of his time Macquarie would have been caught up in the debate about whether the blacks were human. Captain Cook in 1770 looked romantically on the tribes he encountered, writing, 'in reality they are far happier than we Europeans'. Others adopted the tone of English philosopher Thomas Hobbes, who'd claimed that the life of the natives was nasty, brutish and short. Historian Henry Reynolds in *Frontier* reports the attitude of a First Fleet surgeon who wrote that the Aborigines were 'altogether a stupid, insensible set of beings'. George Grey, explorer and later Governor of South Australia, described the blacks as 'occupying a scale in creation which nearly places them on the level of brutes'. By the 1820s a new form of science was in vogue, phrenology, which measured moral and intellectual ability by the shape of the skull. One of the leading phrenologists, George Combe, concluded it was impossible for Aborigines to be civilised because 'the organs reflecting intellect . . . were greatly inferior in size'.

With these prejudices in mind Macquarie looked favourably on the Wiradjuri. One man caught his eye above all others. In his journal of 10 May 1815 he records a meeting with a group of blacks, one of them now believed to be Wiindhuraydhine:

> After breakfasting this morning we were visited by three male natives of the country, all very handsome good-looking young men, and whom we had not seen before. I gave them presents of slops and tomahawks, and to the best looking and stoutest of them I gave a piece of yellow cloth in exchange for his mantle, which he presented me with . . .

So the two chiefs presented each other with gifts. The first meetings between the Wiradjuri and the whites had been peaceful. Macquarie left Bathurst with an order for the men stationed there to treat the blacks well. But another governor, Thomas Brisbane, was soon to rule the colony, and in a few short years Wiindhuraydhine would find himself in irons in prison with his ribs smashed by the muskets of soldiers.

In 1822 the British government drastically reduced the duty on Australian wool. It was a fatal decision for the black tribes west of the Great Dividing Range. Demand for wool from the colony led to a rapid expansion of flocks and people. By 1850 some 200 000 extra British immigrants arrived on these shores. The blacks were overrun. Around Bathurst, 1822 also marked an escalation of violence that would end with Governor Brisbane making war on the Wiradjuri.

Before his resignation, Governor Macquarie made another visit to Bathurst. He reported friendly relations between the blacks and the settlers, and in his journal of December 1821 described a corroboree in his honour which lasted well into the night. Indeed, Wiradjuri people had helped open up the land for the whites. A Wiradjuri man named 'Aaron' forged a path over the mountains to within a short distance of what is now the town of Mudgee. William Lee, one of the earliest settlers, was led by black guides to the Capertee and Bylong valleys. But as the land was gathered up, goodwill turned to animosity, misunderstandings to malevolence. Settler Godfrey Charles Mundy recorded in his book *Our Antipodes* that:

> As our flocks and herds and population increase, and corresponding increase of space is required, the natural owners of the soil are thrust back without treaty, bargain or apology.

The sad but inevitable onset of hostility implicated the families whose names mark so much of the landscape today: William and George Cox, William Lee and the man who'd first led the whites across the mountains, William Lawson. The first serious outbreak of violence was reported at the Cox station on the Cudgegong River. A group of blacks had driven away the stockmen, let loose cattle and killed sheep. Soon after, Lawson reported the killing of one of his own convicts.

In 1823 Major James Thomas Morriset succeeded William Lawson as commandant at Bathurst. Morriset was a military man. Forty-three years old, he'd fought against the French army in Spain. Now he would put the lessons of war to work against the Wiradjuri. In October 1823 Wiindhuraydhine led raids on the properties around Swallow Creek. The attacks were recorded in *Bathurst: 1813 to 1840* by P.N. Long:

> In October and November, natives attacked the stations belonging to Wylde, and Palmer and Marsden, west of Bathurst, scattering the herds, spearing cattle and killing some of the stockmen.

After these attacks Wiindhuraydhine was captured. The *Sydney Gazette* graphically reported his arrest, referring to him by the name often used by the whites, Saturday:

> One of the chiefs (named Saturday) of a desperate tribe took six men to secure him and they had

> actually to break a musket over his body before he yielded, which he did at length with broken ribs.

As the warrior lay in prison, his injuries slowly healing, the whites turned to a new form of warfare. Some settlers took to poisoning food and leaving it for the wandering blacks. Arsenic was used for the treatment of scab in sheep; now it was being laced with flour and the damper or cakes left for the Wiradjuri to eat and die a slow and painful death. The outbreaks of violence were becoming more common.

William Suttor wrote of a settler named Antonio giving some potatoes to a group of blacks passing by. The simple act of kindness triggered a misunderstanding that ended in tragedy.

> Next day they, having appreciated the gift, appeared at a potato patch and commenced to help themselves. This was not to Antonio's liking, who roused the people of the settlement on his behalf. They rushed down and attacked the blacks, some of whom were killed and others maimed.

It was this slaughter that hardened the resolve of Wiindhuraydhine, by now released from prison, to rid the land of the settlers. Surviving the attack, he formed the war party that came on that night to the hut that stands today on Suttor's farm, Brucedale. From there the Wiradjuri leader took his men on the rampage at Millah-Murrah, Mill Post and Warren Gunyah. Now his people were forced to flee under the proclamation of martial law, and a price was on his head.

The reinforcements from the 40th regiment had swelled the local military numbers to seventy-five. The soldiers were augmented by armed locals, and under the command of Major Morriset they were divided into four columns that fanned out across the countryside, with orders to kill the blacks on sight. Heading one of the raiding parties was none other than William Lawson; another was George Rankin. Rankin wrote to his wife on 28 September 1824, lamenting the failure of the mission:

> Yesterday I dined with the commandant after ten days separation in different directions. Major Morriset in the centre with his party went to the north, Mr Walker had command of the left division to the westward, and Mr Lawson and I with the right division to the eastward. None of us succeeded in seeing the enemy, except Walker, and that was in the shape of one black gin and a piccaninny.

The whites scoured a huge area of land. The proclamation of martial law extended at least one hundred miles northwest and south from Bathurst. Despite Rankin's claim not to have seen any blacks, stories of atrocities filtered through. Certainly, numbers of casualties were sometimes exaggerated, but allowing for that there's little doubt large numbers of Aborigines were being killed. In some cases hundreds of blacks were said to be rounded up and shot; women and children driven into deep gorges and massacred. The *Sydney Gazette* of 30 September detailed one battle in which the Wiradjuri fought off the settlers. They were led by a chief known as 'Blucher', who, with two other blacks, was killed before the whites retreated. When the settlers returned the next day they found the Wiradjuri burying their dead. Seizing the weapons of the blacks, they threw them into the fire before slaughtering sixteen of the men.

Major Morriset was determined that blacks would continue to be hunted down and killed until his great foe Wiindhuraydhine was captured. Those who surrendered were promised blankets and food and the chiefs would be presented with badges forged in their honour, but not the notorious 'Saturday'. On 25 August 1824, the Colonial Secretary reissued his public notice for the warrior's capture.

The *Sydney Gazette* continued to cover the futile hunt for Wiindhuraydhine. By 28 October 1824 it reported that 'Saturday . . . still thinks it prudent to keep out of reach and has not even been heard of.' The *Gazette* also carried details of the slow surrender of some of the Wiradjuri. Martial law, though, remained in place. Finally the whites yielded. The man who'd waged war on them for nearly three years, captured once, would not wear the leg-irons of a prisoner again. On 11 December 1824 Governor

Brisbane lifted martial law and sent word of a pardon for Wiindhuraydhine.

The Wiradjuri people were tired and hungry, their numbers were depleted. Mothers had seen their children die; wives and children were left without fathers; those who survived the violence were stricken with diseases they had no resistance to. The Wiradjuri had mounted their last stand; the die was cast. The future was to be one of accommodating the whites; resistance had proven futile. Others would try to defend their lands, and they would meet a similar fate. But the battle of Bathurst would dispel any doubts that Aborigines fought and fought bravely. I know now that my people were not passive, we did not drop our weapons and flee. We were warriors, and there's pride in that.

Wiindhuraydhine knew that leadership was not just about resistance, it was knowing when to stop. If there was to be a surrender, however, it would be surrender with dignity. Two weeks after the lifting of the proclamation of martial law, on 28 December, the two war leaders, Brisbane and Wiindhuraydhine, met for the first time at a great feast at Parramatta, prepared to honour the blacks. Wiindhuraydhine had gathered the last of his people and led them on an epic march for seventeen days across the mountains. Finally, Wiindhuraydhine led 260 Wiradjuri men, women and children into the Parramatta marketplace. The *Sydney Gazette* described him as having a 'noble countenance' with a 'piercing eye', and concluded that he was 'the most manly black native we have ever beheld'. The warrior wore a straw hat fixed with a label carrying the word PEACE. Two days later Governor Brisbane sent a dispatch to London:

> I am most happy to have it in my power to report to your lordship that Saturday, their great and warlike chieftain, has been with me to receive his pardon, and that with most of his tribe attended the annual conference . . .

Now we stand over his grave: the son of settlers and the son of Wiradjuri, white and black, but with a story that unites us. Blood fell on this land, my people fought bravely and without pity. The guns of the whites were turned on my people, the slaughter legally sanctioned, but in battle we found honour; in surrender, dignity and respect. At least a third of the Wiradjuri lost their lives — up to a thousand people. Their sacrifice became the bedrock of our survival today.

'This is like our Lone Pine, isn't it?' I say to John Suttor. The old farmer nods his head.

Wiindhuraydhine enjoyed his peace. His exploits continued to be reported in the colony's newspapers. But the next chapter in the survival of his people would have to be written without him. Wiindhuraydhine died in 1835 from a gangrenous wound suffered in a tribal fight.

The remnants of Wiradjuri society would never again enjoy their sovereignty; our identity would be fashioned as much by our conquerors as our ancestors. The next generation carried the blood of the whites; their descendants, in some cases, would deny Wiindhuraydhine and his people as they sought to 'pass' as whites. As Wiindhuraydhine faded from Australian history the people he led were reduced to begging, living off the hand-outs of the whites, who would take even our names and replace them with theirs. In 1833 the Colonial Secretary recorded the names of Aborigines in the Bathurst district who'd received a ration of blankets. Included in the list were 'Tommy Grant' and 'Jeremy Grant'. My family had their name.

5

Finding Wongamar

The descendants of the Aborigine William Hugh Grant, born 1854 in the Lachlan district, have not established the identity of their forebear.
JACQUELINE GRANT, *PROVIDENCE*

If I'm to believe the man in front of me, his family stole from mine, in some cases killed us. What's more, we share the same name. They've grown fat on land that was once ours, while we've wandered homeless. They've raised their children in freedom, while we've raised ours in the fear, and sometimes the reality, of having them snatched from our arms. One family, one blood; but ours is deemed to be black. In some cases the difference is barely perceptible, but in Australia race is determined under a magnifying glass.

The man shaking my hand owes his good fortune to fate. He was born with the legitimacy of whiteness.

His family photos tell a tale of prosperity, while mine tell of struggle. Pride of place belongs to his great-great-grandfather, John Grant, who is both our common denominator and greatest point of difference. The photo shows a man with a face like a raised scar, all jagged and uneven. If he ever smiled it was so far back in time it no longer registered even as a memory. It's his eyes that draw me in: they're cold and they seem to follow me across the room. But maybe I'm just too used to looking into them, for they're the same eyes I've seen stare back at me from every male member of my family. John was an old man when he posed for this camera, but he was lean and clearly well cared for, not complacent but comfortable. He'd had more sleep-filled nights than restless ones, the sign of a clear conscience, or in his case a ruthless soul. Did the crisp, white bedsheets of his homestead cover the body of a murderer? His soft pillow comforted his head while he wove the dreams that became our nightmares.

'It was the beginning of the great sorrow for your people, when my people came here,' John's great-great-grandson Graham Grant says. 'The old bloke used to hang the blacks, then they made him get a licence for it. It didn't stop him, though.'

If people grow to resemble their land, then Graham Grant is the living proof. Natural selection has erased the Jew and the Irishman and left a quintessential Australian. Not the type of Australian you might find in the city, with their thin lives and faux transatlantic accents; Graham's vowels are flat and he speaks with a nasally upward inflection, the kind you usually hear these days only on grainy black and white newsreel footage. He's fit, a fitness that comes from hard work, not indulgence at a gym. His money, what little there is left of the once bulging family fortune, goes on essentials that clearly don't include regular dental care. His teeth resemble the rusted, chipped blades of a disused hacksaw, but he's not afraid to smile. His matted hair tells you that when he does bother to cut it he stabs away at it himself rather than afford himself the luxury of a ten-dollar barber cut.

Graham Grant greets me with an enthusiasm that would make people in the city cringe. There are no formalities, just a wide open-armed greeting for a long-lost cousin he's never met. We're shackled together, Graham and I, across a divide of race and violence. This is confession time for Graham, who has carried the burden of his family's secrets for too long.

'Come in . . . come in . . . have a cuppa,' Graham says, with such a beaming face you couldn't turn down his offer even if you wanted to.

Graham's boy, Scott, is standing on the verandah. My brother's Scott too. I'm about to learn there are no coincidences in the Grant family. I study Scott's face, searching for resemblance; maybe I'm looking too hard but I'm sure I can see a bit of my cousin Ivan. Graham's wife, Sue, is there to meet me as well. She's the sort of down-to-earth country woman whose life, like her family, is measured by the rhythms of nature. Sue knows there's a time and place for everything.

Generations come and generations go,
but the earth remains forever.
(Ecclesiastes 1:4)

There's another message in the Old Testament book for me and Graham.

I saw the tears of the oppressed —
and they have no comforter;
Power was on the side of their oppressors —
and they have no comforter.
(Ecclesiastes 4:1)

We can't be complete until we are together. What goes for Graham and me goes for this nation, but it's not reconciliation and it's not saying sorry — the solution is found in humility.

'I remember when I was a kid seeing my first black man and I asked Mum what he was,' Graham tells me. 'Anyway, she says, "Well you know how there are black cows and brown cows, Friesians and Brahmans, it's the same with people, but we're all the same inside."' He laughs.

Graham's happiness comes from the suspension of judgment. It's a disarming and endearing quality that allows Graham to speak openly and honestly. It allows him to tell, without any hint of being patronising, how he befriended a little black boy at school. The boy had no shoes so, Graham says, 'I went home and got my spare pair and gave them to him.' This was my chance.

'What did you know about us?' I ask.

'Oh, not much,' he replies, a little vaguely. 'Well, I always knew there were blacks with the name Grant . . . must have been related to us somehow.' Graham speaks slowly. Out here there's nothing but wide open spaces, and I'm not going anywhere, so there's no need to rush.

'I remember once someone said there was a big old black man named Grant; he was a train driver from Sydney and came here to the property and said, "I own a bit of that."'

I don't know who he could mean, but that's hardly surprising; there's no shortage of us. As I've been told too often in my life, we're a bastardised race. I have no claim on any name other than that which is attached to the white blood in my veins. I say attached, because I don't want to pretend there's ever been any sense of family love. Our births weren't planned; we were the unwanted offspring left on history's doorstep. Grant, Coe, Naden, Murray, Sloane, Simpson, Johnson — they're the names that identify the once independent clans of the Wiradjuri people. Now I'm back where it began, on a once vast property known as Merriganowry, with a man named Graham Grant and a photocopy of a brass breastplate inscribed: 'Wongamar, King of the Merriganoury, Back Creek, Konimbla Creek, Lachlan River, John Grant 1847.'

John Grant to Wongamar: two people separated by colour, by land and by culture, who met on the battlefield that was the Australian frontier, but who would be united for an eternity in the blood of their offspring.

The Wiradjuri people were still fighting for their land during the war in Bathurst when an emancipated convict, John Grant, first appeared to stake his claim and make his fortune in 1823. Just a few years later the bedraggled Wiradjuri survivors were pushed to the fringes of society by settlers like John Grant who eagerly swallowed up the land to run more sheep and cattle. The early signs of a debilitating welfare dependency were to be seen in the blankets and rations handed out by a colonial government satisfying its conscience that it was at least doing something for the natives. Only ten years later, in 1836, Charles Darwin, visiting Bathurst, would write:

> The number of Aborigines is rapidly decreasing. This decrease, no doubt, must be partly owing to the introduction of spirits, to European diseases, even the milder ones of which, such as measles, prove very destructive, and to the gradual extinction of the wild animals.

The land was still being opened up at the point of a gun. The blacks, wherever they could, continued to resist. An old verse recounts how one settler, John Collitts, was driven from Bangaroo station, right next door to where Grant would establish his property, Merriganowry.

With spears and woomeras and boomerangs too,
They hunted poor Johnny from Bangaroo,
And Hannah and Bridget and children too,
Were forced to flee from Bangaroo.

Occasionally a ray of hope would shine through the gloom, as benevolence ruled over terror. On the Suttor property at Brucedale, by then the burial ground of Wiindhuraydhine, blacks were employed as stockmen. But families like the Suttors were all too few. In his diaries of the 1830s–40s, explorer Sir Thomas Mitchell provided a grim view of life on the frontier, describing the blacks' fear of the redcoats. There is a glimpse of how quickly and brutally the tragedy unfolded in the contact between Mitchell and a black man known as Bultje, whom he often used as a guide. Bultje was a leader of his people, and on one occasion helped ease tensions between the blacks and Mitchell's men. Eleven years later, Mitchell returned and found that his old friend had been killed. In fact almost all of the men of Bultje's clan were dead and the women taken as servants and sexual partners for station hands.

Atrocities against blacks often happened out of sight of the authorities, making it difficult to obtain enough legal proof to bring charges. But the terror passed into folklore and is repeated today by the descendants of pioneer families. The Grants were no different. As a child, Graham was taken into the confidence of his old great-aunt, Ethel, who whispered a sickening deathbed confession she wanted to be purged of before she faced her judgment. Ethel, as a young girl, had been told to lace with arsenic the blacks' ration of flour.

'I told your Uncle Cecil and Aunty Flo about this,' Graham says. 'But it was a bit hard for them to take. I feel I can tell you, you're not so caught up in it,' he adds.

Hard to take. Am I supposed to just shrug this off? Is it my duty to forgive and forget? Surely the sins of the father are not so easily excused. But I haven't come for recrimination. I want the Grants to acknowledge just one thing: we are the same as them. I want to reclaim our honour. If what we've been told is true, the blood of John Grant, a man who took the land and killed my people, runs through my veins.

The story of my family is played out among the rolling hills of what is now known as 'Cabonne Country, the Nation's Food Basket'. The rich soil of the region attracted the settlers from around Bathurst and the lower Blue Mountains who were battling a drought. In the summer of 1826–27, John Grant gathered seventeen men, 1000 head of cattle and seven flocks of sheep, each numbering between 500 and 1000, and settled on fertile flats along the Lachlan River. He would, in time, become the richest Catholic in the colonies, a far cry from the young rebel Irishman who only fifteen years before had been sentenced to hang.

County Tipperary in 1810 was a place of terror for Irish Catholics. The Grants of Moyne were farmers under the tyranny of English landlords. They had at one time been members of the aristocracy, their line tracing back to 940 in Florence. Otto Gherardini had been a mercenary soldier and his wanderings took him to Normandy, where his descendants went by the name 'Le Grande'. They came to England with William the Conqueror and adapted their name to 'Le Grant', and eventually to 'Grant'. In 1170 the Grants were among the first Normans to arrive in Ireland, becoming the Barons of Iverk in Kilkenny, but they were dispossessed by Oliver Cromwell's forces. The many branches of the Grant tree are documented today by Monsignor Leo Grant, a Catholic priest in Bathurst. He tells me that after Cromwell the Grants became 'flotsam on the sea of Irish history, every generation being forced to move on by famine or civil unrest'.

In 1810 the Grants were to become entangled with Gilbert Maher, a man described as 'one of the most despised and vindictive landlords in Moyne'. It was a crossing of paths that was to end in bloodshed, execution and transportation to the penal colony of New South Wales, so beginning a chain of events that places me here today. John Grant was just seventeen years old when he was led by his older brother, Jeremiah, into the secret societies plotting the overthrow of 'landlordism'. The Irish Catholic faith was not officially recognised, and like many others the Grants lived under a curfew. Anyone found to have broken it could be transported without trial. Jeremiah was known as one of the county's leading young rebels. A book written in 1816, *The Life and Adventures of Jeremiah Grant*, describes him as tall, athletic, with thick black shining hair. It says, 'He neither represented a Hercules nor an Apollo Belvedere, but he was between both.' The praise, though, was tempered with this warning: 'This illiterate pedagogue was incapable of correcting animal passions, and utterly destitute of mental powers.'

Jeremiah and his followers targeted Gilbert Maher and victimised anyone who tried to deal with the landlord. James Shea discovered just how determined Jeremiah Grant could be. Shea had leased some of Maher's land at Lisanure and was quickly warned by the rebels of the dire consequences if he didn't get off it. The warning was posted on the chapel door at Tempeltuohy on 23 March 1810:

> Don't be mistaken James Shea, if you keep Lisanure your own place will be destroyed, it's not yours but any person that takes one sod of Gilbert Henry Maher's ground in this County, we now advize the publick . . . by the holy man that created this day, if any persons should be so headstrong as to take any part of the Villain's ground in this County, before they will hold it one month they will meet their fate, April 23 1810, for in the first place we will trough the stock and poison the ground and if that don't do, we know how to manage after, and be it known that it won't be children's work.

On 3 May 1810, Shea's home was burnt to the ground.

Jeremiah Grant at this time was already on the run, spending most of 1809 in the secret hideouts and tunnels of a graveyard next to an old church. He was being hunted for the attempted murder of Gilbert Maher's agent, a man called Gleeson. Jeremiah had been living with his wife and seven children on a farm leased from Maher. He had received an inheritance from his uncle, and his wife, Anne, had come from a wealthy family, but Maher accused Grant of failing to meet the terms of his tenancy. *The Life and Adventures of Jeremiah Grant* describes Maher as a 'man of malevolence . . . enabled to oppress his tenants, under the colour of justice'. Maher issued a warrant of distress on Jeremiah and sent Gleeson to sell up Grant's stock and household goods to reclaim rent in arrears. A fist fight broke out, then Jeremiah aimed a pistol at Gleeson. It misfired but the agent reported the attack to Maher, who had Grant charged.

With Jeremiah a fugitive, the Maher family hatched a plan of seduction they hoped would lead to betrayal. Gilbert Maher's son, Nicholas, began a relationship with Jeremiah's sister, Mary. She was married, but her husband had deserted her and she was living with her mother, Eleanor. Learning of the affair, Jeremiah was outraged. Nicholas Maher, he said:

> . . . succeeded as was reported, not without force, in violating her chastity, and what is more to be lamented, not only polluted her person, but

> debauched her morals, expelling every principle of virtue from her heart . . .

Jeremiah should have shown less concern for his sister's morality and more for her treachery! With her mind 'depraved by passion and attachment to vicious sensuality', Mary entered into a conspiracy against both Jeremiah and her younger brother, John. Together she and Nicholas concocted a story that John had fired a gun at the young Maher as he rode one night from his father's house. They claimed that John yelled out, 'I am sorry I missed you!'

John was arrested the next day, and Mary then told her lover where the police could find the fugitive Jeremiah. With the two young rebels in prison, Nicholas Maher cooled his relationship with Mary Grant. Mary was furious. 'Her pride was hurt; and the corrodings of jealousy stung her brain almost to madness.' To this was added an overwhelming guilt for the plight of her brothers. Nicholas was the only witness against John, and Mary was determined that he wouldn't live long enough to stand in the witness box. With her mother's encouragement, Mary lured Maher to her hut. According to Jeremiah:

> Under the pretence of renovating love, she decoyed him to her bed, and when [he was] sunk in sleep and inebriety, she became an assassin, and with a heavy stone beat out his devoted brains.

Nicholas Maher's body was found dumped in a nearby field, his face bashed almost beyond recognition. A trail of blood followed from the Grants' hut, and witnesses told of finding Eleanor Grant sitting on a bloodstained mat. Nicholas's father, the landlord Gilbert Maher, implicated the entire Grant family in the killing. Mary and Eleanor, as well as John, Jeremiah and even Jeremiah's wife, Anne, were charged with the murder. Jeremiah and Anne managed to argue an acquittal; Eleanor was found guilty but later discharged from prison; Mary was found guilty and executed. John, too, had been found guilty and sentenced to hang, but the sentence was commuted to transportation for life to New South Wales. He wouldn't soon forget his sister, however, and her name would become a vital clue in the search for my ancestors.

Much of John Grant's story is told in the book *Providence*, by Jacqueline Grant, the wife of one of John's descendants. It tells how John Grant was eighteen years old when the ship *Providence* sailed into Sydney Cove on Tuesday, 2 July 1811. He was one of 180 convicts held in irons who'd sailed for 162 days to meet their fate in a new land. Here, the young John would find Catholics to be as despised as they had been back home in Ireland. The Reverend Samuel Marsden had campaigned against the growing influence of Irish Catholicism. He described Irish Catholics as ignorant, uncivilised savages, lacking any real religion or morality. Governor Hunter, in 1796, had described them as turbulent and worthless creatures, and wished they'd 'either been sent to the coast of Africa, or some place as fit for them'. The young rebel, John Grant, would have been among the generation of Irish convicts who saw themselves as doubly colonised. An Irish Catholic convict could take meagre comfort only from the fact that at least he wasn't black. As Robert Hughes concluded in *The Fatal Shore*, his landmark convict history:

> Galled by exile, the lowest of the low, they desperately needed to believe in a class inferior to themselves. The Aborigines answered that need. Australian racism began with the convicts . . .

Indeed, John Grant's greatest blessing in his new land was his white skin. Whatever iniquities he would endure, it was the one thing he could be certain would not inhibit his social and economic mobility.

For Wongamar it was to be a far more bleak fate. The young Wiradjuri man was still living a life his people had enjoyed for two thousand generations. They occupied an area of land larger than England, extending from the Blue Mountains as far west as Hay, north to Dubbo and south along the Murray River to Albury. The population of the Wiradjuri was estimated as between three and five thousand. The people divided themselves into clans, tightknit family structures, but were united in a common language. Wongamar had grown to manhood respecting the power of Baiami, the great father. Like other boys of his clan, he would have entered a world of great magic and mystery, learning the secrets of his people in an ancient ritual — the Burrbang — in which he'd be made into a man. This was the world he understood; Wongamar would have had no idea that he was also a British subject.

As the ships of the First Fleet sailed into Botany Bay, the local Eora people yelled 'Warra-warra', which translates as 'Go away', or 'Leave!'. Yet in the eyes of the law the Wiradjuri people, along with the more than six hundred similar tribes on the continent, did not exist. Captain Cook, eighteen years earlier, had claimed this land for Britain, declaring it *terra nullius*, an empty land. The Supreme Court of New South Wales in 1836 would articulate this fiction, with Justice Burton delivering a judgment in *R v Murrel* that the Aborigines:

> . . . had not attained at the first settlement to such a position in point of numbers, and civilisation, and to such a form of government and laws, as to be entitled to be recognised as so many sovereign states governed by the laws of their own.

For the purposes of Australian settlement, blacks simply had no rights.

British rule not only denied Wongamar's property inheritance, it rendered any resistance to the invasion of his land a criminal act. He and his countrymen would be seen not as fighters in the defence of their land and culture, but as crude, vicious murderers. Peace was a vain hope. As the colony's first governor, Captain Arthur Phillip, soon discovered, war was an inevitability that overwhelmed even the most seemingly noble aspirations. At first, Phillip attempted friendship with the people he met at Botany Bay, offering beads and ribbon. In one exchange, an ironic foretaste of the degradation to come, Lieutenant Philip Gidley King gave two Aborigines a taste of wine, which they spat out. Phillip had issued strict orders that the natives not be offended or molested, and should be treated with friendship. His kindly intentions, however, were soon shown to be very much overstated. Henry Reynolds in *Frontier* writes:

> Phillip's record regarding the Aborigines is less impressive than traditional accounts suggest. There were at least two instances when military parties fired indiscriminately into groups of Aborigines and four other occasions when troops were sent out with the intention of 'making a severe example of them' . . .

One of those examples involved the pursuit of the infamous black resistance leader Pemulwuy, who'd speared Phillip's gamekeeper, a convict named McEntire. The governor was outraged and sent Captain Watkin Tench on a punitive raid with instructions to capture two members of the clans around Botany Bay and to kill ten others whose heads were to be chopped off and carried into the settlement. Tench later had the orders modified: to capture six, execute some and send the others back to spread the lesson. That Tench and his party failed to find Pemulwuy and his men did nothing to lessen the hostile intent.

As British subjects, blacks were to be extended the full protection of the law. The local people, however, would hardly have been reassured as they witnessed the behaviour of the whites. Only weeks after the fleet landed they would have heard screams and rushed to witness an orgy the likes of which they could probably scarcely comprehend. Arthur Bowes-Smythe, the surgeon on the female transport vessel, *Lady Penrhyn*, recorded in his journal of 6 February 1788: 'It is beyond my abilities to give a just description of the scene of debauchery and riot that ensued during the night.' The blacks would also have seen, in the first weeks of settlement, drunkenness and fighting, the first floggings and the first hanging.

With the law turning a blind eye to the recognition of black rights, another fiction was taking root in this land — the belief that Australian settlement was an essentially benign and peaceful process. By the 1880s Percy Russell composed a poem celebrating the achievements of his land:

Her shield unsullied by a single crime,
Her wealth of gold and still more golden fleece,
Forth stands Australia, in her birth sublime,
The only nation from the womb of peace.

This convenient reading of history persisted throughout my own schooling, the story of my people reduced to little more than a footnote. Indeed, it wasn't until 1968 that the enlightened anthropologist W.E.H. Stanner, delivering a Boyer lecture, held this nation to account for what he termed the 'great Australian silence'. Yet in the early days, the colony was anything but silent about the treatment of blacks. War is a word used with much reluctance even today, yet that's precisely the language that was used in the nineteenth century. Reynolds asks the question: Was it warfare? He cites the missionary L.E. Threlkeld in 1826: 'You will be grieved to hear that war has commenced and still continues against the Aborigines of this land.' A settler in 1839 wrote that Aborigines were 'enemies arrayed in arms and waging war against Europeans as their invaders'. Watkin Tench, too, claimed Governor Phillip was 'tired of this state of petty warfare and endless uncertainty'. Some were already expressing guilt. E.W. Landor in *The Bushman, or Life in a New Country* wrote:

> We have seized upon this country and shot the inhabitants, until the survivors have found it expedient to submit to our rule. We have acted exactly as Julius Caesar did when he took possession of Britain. But Caesar was not so hypocritical as to pretend any moral right to possession.

Thus, on Tuesday, 2 July 1811, on the banks of the Lachlan River, my two ancestors — John Grant, an

Irish Catholic convict, and Wongamar, a young Wiradjuri man — were unalterably placed on a collision course that would find me following their tracks nearly two hundred years later.

John Grant was a product of his time, shaped by the forces at play in his home of Ireland and in his new land. As Jacqueline Grant tells it, back home he'd rebelled against British tyranny; indeed martial law had been declared against his people in 1797. His family had been part of the great rebellion in 1798, and like all survivors counted themselves lucky not to have been among the 30 000 people cut down in the space of just a few weeks. This was a man all too familiar with terror, yet here he would reap its benefits as the blacks suffered the same fate his countrymen had endured. The oppressed so quickly becomes the oppressor.

As pointed out in *Providence*, it was the massacre of Aborigines near Dr William Redfern's property, Campbellfield, in the Western Sydney district that provided a reversal of fortune for John Grant. The Gandangara people had attacked and killed some workmen and children as payback for the murder of their own people by whites. In March 1816 they came again in search of food with their neighbours, the Tharawal, and attacked and killed more settlers. Samuel Hassal and Robert Lowe, a local magistrate, took the law into their own hands, gathering forty men and arming them with pitchforks, pistols and muskets.

The vigilantes were unsuccessful, but after the blacks launched more attacks in the Appin and Airds districts,

Governor Macquarie instructed Captain James Wallis of the 46th regiment to hunt them down and kill them, making no distinction between hostile or friendly natives. Matthew McAllister was William Redfern's overseer, and reported seeing the blacks on his property. Captain Wallis rushed to the area, but finding no sign of his foe, nor of McAllister, suspected the overseer of sending him on a wild-goose chase to provide sanctuary for the blacks. Wallis eventually found a group of Gandangara camping at Appin, and without warning he had his men open fire, slaughtering as many as they could. Those who survived were so terrified they rushed to their deaths over nearby cliffs. While it could not be proved that McAllister had tried to save the blacks, by the end of the year he was no longer at Campbellfield. In his place was John Grant.

Grant proved himself a man with an eye for the main chance. As overseer, he grew close to William Redfern. Whether it was a relationship born of real affection or of opportunism, the result was the same. By 1828 the former convict would hold more land and livestock assets than any other Catholic, free or freed, in the colony. As Redfern increased his holdings, so did Grant. He's acknowledged as the founder of the Blue Mountains town of Hartley, and he also established Canowindra along the fertile banks of the Lachlan and Belabula Rivers. Grant, free of the shackles of servitude, soon aspired to authority, with Redfern, also a magistrate, appointing him a constable in the Campbelltown district. The one-time

Irish rebel was serving the very same Crown he had fought to overthrow.

Grant the squatter proved himself a tough master. Between 1836 and 1839 he brought twenty proceedings before the magistrate at Hartley against his assigned convicts. On 4 December 1836, William Chalmers was sentenced to fifty lashes for stealing tools from Grant. In another case James Mackey received seventy-five lashes for neglect of duty. Resenting the punishment, Mackey armed himself with a stolen musket and tried to kill Grant; for that his sentence was increased to life. Things had indeed turned full circle: John Grant, sent to the colony for his involvement in the murder of his landlord's son, was himself a figure to be feared and despised.

By 1832 Grant was a widower with three young children and had staked out the land where he would establish the vast property he named Merriganowry, on the Lachlan. John's wife, a former convict named Jane O'Brien, had died six years earlier. His son, Jeremiah, remained with his father, but the girls, Mary and Eleanor, were cared for by William Redfern's wife, Sarah. In the years after his wife's death, Grant had forged a path deeper into the plains west of the mountains. He's been described as a man of great initiative, tough-minded and resourceful. He could also be justly described as one of the men who 'pretended a moral right' to the land. Wherever Grant found land, there were already people on it. When he settled Merriganowry, Wongamar and his people posed no obstacle. They lived on the land, but to Grant it was his for the taking. So too, it seems, were the black women — including Wongamar's daughter.

'Father: John Grant (squatter).' It was this entry in my great-grandfather Bill Grant's marriage certificate, dated 8 July 1878, that convinced my family that John Grant was indeed our ancestor. Bill Grant is one of those mysterious figures who moves so softly on this land they leave barely a trace. His marriage certificate makes no mention of his mother, and when he died on 27 December 1939 his mother and father were listed as unknown. In his eighty-three years William Hugh Grant would father fifteen children to two women; he lived in two worlds, one white, one black; he was said to have the powers of the old Wiradjuri 'clever men', the ability to heal, to hypnotise and even to seemingly fly through the air, yet today no-one can tell me even what he looked like and there are no photographs. If he was the child of John Grant, then it was a birth 'from the wrong side of the sheets', with no official mention in any family tree. Still, there were clues, just enough for me to finally answer the question: who was Bill Grant?

'He looks just like Cecil,' Mum said, referring to the uncanny likeness between this man and my dad's brother.

We all rushed to the window to peep outside and see an old white man walking up our driveway. Only this wasn't a white man, no matter how light his skin was, he was one of us. His grandfather was Bill Grant, his father and my father's father were brothers. To look at Dad with his black skin and broad flat nose you may not think it, but they were first cousins. Don was on a journey, a journey to heal the wounds of his past and find his family. Like so many of my people, his was a life cheated by a society that encouraged light-skinned blacks to hide the family photos when guests came around. Don discovered he was black in a pub in Cowra. He'd grown up white, with a white mother and a white father — one who looked white anyway — and Don had grown up, he's ashamed to say, a racist.

'After a few beers, I started mouthing off about the blacks,' Don said. It was then that one of his friends interrupted him and told him he shouldn't be talking like that because, 'Don't you know, you're a blackfella.' Don rushed home and confronted his father.

'Mum rushed out of the room and at first Dad didn't want to admit it, until I forced it out of him,' Don said.

Don had always been told that his grandfather, Bill Grant, was dead. Now his father, Henry, admitted he'd been alive and living on the Cowra mission when Don was a boy.

'My father used to visit the mission every weekend, taking groceries and clothes over. He told me it was for the blacks, but I know now he was going to see his father,' Don said.

These are the hard choices that shame demands of us. Don said he felt cheated; well so do we. Don's family were conveniently white when it mattered; when the choice was flight or fight they chose their side. Are we not entitled to think they're equally conveniently black — is that too harsh? Yet there's another side of me that says Don's family had no choice. Now he had come among us to meet my grandmother and to put himself back together, to begin his own search for his grandfather Bill — and for Wongamar.

Bill Grant was born on the Lachlan River at North Logan near Cowra, probably in 1857. We have no way of knowing for sure because, like so many other blacks, his birth was not recorded. He would have been just another of the Wiradjuri kids born on the Grants' Merriganowry, except for the colour of his skin, made a golden brown by the white blood in his veins. Perhaps old Wongamar looked at him and saw in the boy the face of the station boss; the women giggling and whispering among themselves about little Bill's true father. As a child I remember my father would drive with me past Merriganowry and tell me how 'old Grandfather', as he called him, was raised there. The young Bill certainly lived and worked on the property and even gained an education, reading and writing fluently. When he was in his early twenties he and a local white girl, Margaret Brien, ran off to Grenfell to secretly marry. Margaret was only thirteen years old, and married to a black man she was cut off from her family and excluded from her father's will.

Bill continued to live and work around the Grant property. He and Margaret had eleven children. Like all other blacks he was under the control of the ironically named Aborigines Protection Board, an agency set up to supposedly smooth the dying pillow of a doomed race. On 16 May 1892, the board noted an application by 'William Grant, an Aboriginal', for a grant of land at Cowra. My family have long maintained Bill had been given some land by the Grant family, and his successful application to the Protection Board would seem to confirm it. A half-white Aborigine, married to a white woman with so-called quarter-caste kids, would have been well on the way to becoming respectable, but for Bill, living in two worlds wouldn't last.

By the turn of the century Bill had left Margaret Brien and was living with an Aboriginal woman, Catherine Ryan, and her children on the Bulgandramine Mission at Peak Hill, near Dubbo. Bill and Catherine would have four children of their own, including my grandfather Cecil William Henry Grant.

Bill's former wife remained in Cowra, her younger children kept apart from their black relatives. They buried their secret with successive marriages into the local white community. There their shame would be hidden until Don bravely searched for the truth. I'm told Margaret Brien died never having forgiven her ex-husband. So a schism grew in the family, and it has never been resolved.

The worlds of the black Grants and their white cousins grew steadily further apart. My grandfather, Cecil, married an Aboriginal woman, Josie Johnson, from Condobolin, and had my father and his four brothers and sisters. We were Grant by name, but black in our souls. The truth, though, was hidden in the names: names like William and Henry, Stan, Florence, James and Catherine, names that would appear over and over, both in my family and the official Grant family tree, names that would lead me back to John Grant and to Wongamar. On my search, I had come with so many questions. And each person seemed to provide another piece to the puzzle. Two names stand out above all others in my search: Selina and Mary.

The old woman knew. I walked into the local museum in Canowindra and she knew what I was there for. This was my home and finally I was about to reclaim my heritage.

'They used them and abused them,' she said.

The grey-haired white lady was my cousin. The truth of her black relatives had been kept from her as she had been kept from us. She knew nothing of Bill and his two wives — one white, one black — but she didn't doubt that her ancestors had used mine as surely as they'd taken our land. Now I was back in a town that had changed little since my great-grandfather Bill walked these same streets. I passed the same trees he'd have sought shade under in the summer; the same water ran in the rivers and creeks he would have swum in and drunk from; the same stars shone down on us at night. The old store, Finns, had been built when Bill was a boy, and I wondered if he had leant on its rails. Had he stood outside as the locals whispered, 'There's that half-caste boy, they say he's one of the Grants.' Bill was talking to me. The man my father told me could speak to our minds and send messages across great distances wanted me to know the truth.

Madeline Forgey and Alma Cowley live with ghosts. Each day these women travel in time to speak to people long gone from this earth, and the dead give up their secrets. When I visited the two amateur historians in Cowra, my ancestors were ready to reveal themselves to me. Expecting my visit, Madeline and Alma had pulled the file marked 'Grant'. It told a by now familiar tale: John Grant married to Jane O'Brien, three children, Jeremiah, Mary and Eleanor; second marriage to Elizabeth West and nine more children. There was a John junior, a Thomas, another Mary, but no William. John was an old man of sixty-one when his last child, a daughter, Jane, was born in 1853.

John's second wife, Elizabeth, was twenty years younger than her husband when they married in 1833. Sarah Redfern, the wife of John's old boss, Dr William

Redfern, had urged him to remarry or she would take his two daughters with her to England. John had been a widower for seven years and in that time had become a man of property and wealth, but Mrs Redfern was concerned about his lifestyle. Elizabeth West was of 'pure merino' stock, a Protestant whose family were free settlers. By marrying her, John Grant's transformation from convict to gentleman was complete. But what of Mrs Redfern's concerns about the welfare of John's children? What of the seven years the wealthy squatter had spent supposedly alone? The Grants bury their dead carefully; if there was a clue I wouldn't find it easily.

'Are there any other names you can think of?' asked Madeline, when we couldn't find any record of Bill Grant in the Grant file.

'We could try the Watt family,' I replied.

John's eldest daughter, Mary, had married William Redfern Watt, a nephew of Dr William Redfern. They had six children, including sons named William and Hugh. I reminded myself that Great-grandfather Bill was named William Hugh. The link, in my mind, was undeniable, but there were just too many loose ends. Mary's boy William had been born in 1847, Hugh in 1855. They were the grandsons of old John, who was sixty-three when he held Hugh in his arms, and Bill would not be born for another two years. Would a 65-year-old man, already with twelve children and twenty grandchildren; father yet another child? Could the John Grant listed as father on Bill's marriage certificate be, in fact, John junior, child of John and his second wife, Elizabeth West? He'd have been twenty-two when Bill was born, certainly a more likely age than his father, and he was also by then married to Julia Finn and had two children, yet another John and Mary. There was no record of a child called William. It doesn't make it impossible, but the official family files would not easily betray their authors.

'Have you looked at the old unmarked graves list?' Madeline Forgey refused to give up.

'Do you have them?' I asked.

Madeline and Alma looked at each other and smiled. They'd painstakingly gone back over the old register in the courthouse, matching death records with the unmarked mounds in the cemetery. They enjoyed surprising people like me, and they were rightly proud of their work. Alma pulled the book from its shelf and handed it to me. 'They're in alphabetical order.'

I thumbed through the entries under 'G', looking for a name, a clue, anything that might end my search. My eyes fell on a Bertha Grant, a little girl who died in 1889 only five weeks old; her parents were my great-grandfather William Grant and his young white wife, Margaret Jane Brien. Little Bertha would have been my dad's aunty. The human waste is heartbreaking. How many lives were cut short? How many brothers never knew their sisters?

But there was nothing here to help me discover who Bill's father was. I thumbed through the lists, stopping on the name 'Glass'. The Glass family had been settlers working for John Grant and there were many

Aborigines who'd adopted the name. I remembered that Bill's marriage to young Margaret had been witnessed with an 'X' by John and Selina Glass. There it was! Selina Jane Glass, died 2 May 1898, aged fifty-two years. There was more: her father was a man known only by his surname, Gray, but her mother was Mary Ann Grant. Selina had married a man named John Glass. My family had always maintained that Selina was great-grandfather Bill's sister. Now I had confirmation that her mother was a Grant.

I quickly did my sums. If Selina was fifty-two when she died in 1898, she'd have been born in 1846 or early 1847. The official Grant family tree did show a Mary Anne, but she was born in 1842, and was clearly not Selina's mother. But the recurrence of family names was uncanny. Old John Grant already had a daughter, Mary, born to his first wife and named after his sister, and he had another daughter called Mary Anne, born to his second wife. In 1851 his daughter Eleanor had a child she named Selina, and John's youngest daughter was Jane, after his first wife, Jane O'Brien. Yes, it was confusing. But by putting the names and dates together, I'd found a map to my family's past. I continued to count off the dates. John would have been well in his fifties and married to Elizabeth West when Selina was born, but what of Selina's mother, the mysterious Mary Ann Grant? Allowing for her to be around eighteen when she gave birth to Selina, that would put Mary Ann's date of birth somewhere around 1828. John Grant was by then a widower and roaming the land between Bathurst and Cowra staking his fortune. The official colonial records show blacks with the name 'Grant' receiving blankets and rations from the 1830s. Slowly an answer emerged. John Grant could have been Mary Ann's father and Bill's grandfather. Who was Mary Ann's mother? My family's oral history tells me she was Wongamar's daughter.

The unmarked graves list read like a family history. 'Goolagong, Caroline. Died 27 July 1899, aged twenty-six years. Daughter of John Coe and Elizabeth Grant (Aborigine), married Richard Goolagong.' Elizabeth Grant? That name again. A quick calculation put her birth somewhere around 1853, in between the birth of Selina Jane and William Hugh; yet another sister? Another world was being revealed, a world where black and white lived on the same land, carried the same names, but hid the truth from each other. Merriganowry was starting to resemble a plantation from the American south, where 'Massa' had his way with the black slaves, creating an antebellum caste system with his coffee-coloured offspring serving at the table of his Georgian manor. There were other parallels with American slavery. Aborigines Bill Grant, his mother, Mary Ann, and old Wongamar before them, had begun to fall into paternalistic relationships with the white boss. Wongamar and his people could stay on the land and maintain their lifestyle, but only if they accepted John Grant as boss. John Grant the Irishman now owned this land and everything on it — including, it seems, the women.

The 'white' Grants have long denied our blood ties. In her book *Providence*, Jacqueline Grant dismisses us in a footnote, as 'having not established the identity of their forebear'. Her family's silence and a lack of official government records for Aborigines have made that possible. What I do have is my family's word, and now a daisy chain of dates and names that show how John Grant, squatter, built his wealth and power as he filled up his property with his black children and grandchildren, half-brothers and sisters of his legitimate children. He even gave them the same names.

There were still many questions. Did the black Mary Ann work for her white sister Mary, tending her boys William and Hugh? Is that why she named her boy William Hugh? And if John was not William's father, but grandfather, who was his father? Was it the unknown man Gray who apparently fathered Selina? Certainly there are as many black Grays today as there are black Grants. Selina, Elizabeth, William — how many other children might Mary Ann have had? My father tells me about growing up in Condobolin with his uncles, Jack and Jerry Grant, and his aunty, Lizzie. Yes, there were holes, but when I thanked Madeline and Alma, I left satisfied.

The old man Wongamar had seen his land stolen, his people shot down and poisoned and his daughter give birth to a white man's child. In return he got a brass breastplate and a mocking title: 'King of the Merriganourie'. He lies in an unmarked grave, covered by weeds and the passing of time. There is not even a sign now of where it is. John Grant, the Irish rebel and convict who became a gentleman, is buried beneath an enormous headstone on the land he claimed as his own.

Perhaps I've defamed his memory; there's no way of knowing for sure. No-one bothered to keep accurate records of our births or deaths; John Grant could rule with impunity. I have the fact of my birth and the stories of my family; now I also have the confession of a man who wants to rid himself of the Grant inheritance of lies and deception. To defend old John Grant is to say that our pain doesn't matter, that our lives are not worth as much.

What happened here happened to us all. I came to Merriganowry with questions and I left with answers; but meaning still eludes me. Perhaps the answer is in the Bible that John Grant brought with him to his new land; the harsh scripture of an Irish Catholic who saw tryanny and became a tyrant.

> *In the place of judgement —*
> *wickedness was there,*
> *in the place of justice —*
> *wickedness was there.*
> *(Ecclesiastes 3: 16)*

My only comfort is that it is true that the dead are happier than the living, and 'better than both is he who has not yet been born, who has not seen the evil that is done under the sun'.

6

Madmen, Missionaries and Misfits

Ah, when will the time come that these our children of the forest are exalted with the hope that Christianity inspires?

REV JAMES GUNTHER'S DIARY

Her name was Rachael, that's all we know. Yet her story reaches across the years to speak to us today, to tell us of a society that was imploding in the face of white violence and exploitation; of black men who'd lost all self-respect; and of the most victimised of all, black women who were sold by their husbands to white men who raped and abused them, left them riddled with disease. Rachael's story is also the tale of half-caste children, consigned to a life of rejection by the very society that created them. Rachael's screams echo still in the lives of so many Aboriginal mothers, sisters and daughters.

What a pitiful, sad turn of fate it is that history records her name at all. Murder distinguished Rachael from her countrymen — a seemingly barbaric, incomprehensible but, to her, sickeningly necessary murder. How much better it would've been for her had she joined the hundreds of thousands of her people wiped from the pages of the Australian legend, relegated at best to a footnote. But even among a people so degraded, Rachael was destined to be one of the unlucky ones. Her crime, committed in the wilds of the frontier, would be whispered in the halls of the British House of Commons.

'Have you any other facts to state with respect to any other settlement? With respect to New Holland?'

The question, apparently innocuous, was uttered with all of the subtlety expected of the gentlemen heading the select committee's inquiry into the treatment of native peoples. The questioner, so accustomed to having his sensitivities bludgeoned by the endless reports of wanton colonial cruelty in South Africa, North America, New Zealand and Australia, could not help but be shocked by the answer.

> These perhaps do not fall strictly within the terms of the question, namely 'acts of cruelty and oppression'. They relate to the pernicious influence of the immoral conduct of the European upon the natives . . . They are taken from the journals of the Reverend W. Watson, a missionary of the Church Missionary Society, stationed at Wellington Valley,

> New South Wales, and relate to the illicit intercourse of Europeans with the female Aborigines. This is a source of the most afflictive and distressing consequences, and leads, I am afraid, beyond all question, to infanticide to a considerable extent.

Infanticide. Babies, in the first hour of life, taken into the scrub and murdered. Distraught young mothers wailing as they used rocks to cave in their babies' skulls. This was the pitiful testimony of the Reverends John Beecham and William Ellis to the inquiry in London in 1836. They told of a people in decay, stripped of their land, denied legal and civil rights, prey to the abuses of their tormentors, the white settlers. These people had become part of a social experiment aimed at 'civilising and Christianising'. Yet the self-appointed protectors of the blacks could do nothing to shield the objects of their pity from the evil of settlers who saw the Aborigines as barely human. The missions had plunged into despair, and a clash of cultures was played out with devastating, heartbreaking effect.

Barely twenty years had passed since the Wiradjuri people had first laid eyes on a white man when the girl known only as Rachael found herself pregnant to one. Hers was a society in a sorry transition: Rachael was part of the old ways, one of a people for whom the whites had already prophesied extinction, and her unborn child conceived in exploitation and violence faced a life disconnected from its past and locked out of its country's future. Death, in these circumstances, could be seen less as a tragedy and almost as a deliverance. No mother should ever experience the anguish Rachael endured, giving birth to a child whose fight for life, whose gasp for air, would be in vain, whose very first cry would be its last. Rachael knew what she must do, and the threats of missionary Reverend William Watson would do nothing to stop her. What happened next was recorded in Reverend Watson's diary and read out to the gentlemen of the House of Commons:

> At this station I saw Rachael, the gin (or wife) of Bobby, King of Wellington, who expects every hour to be delivered; she was in the hut attended by a black female and an old man whom they named the doctor. She was here a short time ago, and I warned her not to kill the child when it should be born; she promised that she would not. The man at the hut informs me that several blacks . . . persuaded her to go into the bush, that the child might be destroyed as soon as it made its appearance.

Rachael's child would never carry its father's name. The local stockman named Kelley saw no reason to feel responsible for his child. As for Rachael, Kelley had bought her from King Bobby for the price of a few handkerchiefs. Of the child all that's known is what the old women told Reverend Watson: 'He was narrang [little] white and narrang black.' Other children were to meet a similar fate. In his diary entry of 27 April 1833 Watson tells of coming across a group of women in the act of killing a baby:

> . . . we perceived by the light of the fire a white infant laid very near to it, and apparently struggling in the agonies of death, but not crying. The elder yeenur [woman] was sitting with her back to it, and the younger yeenur was digging a hole in the ground with a long stick . . . Mrs W asked why she had killed the child. She said, 'Not very good that one, this one very good,' taking the black child Charlotte and putting it to her breast. Mrs W asked if she had killed the child with the staff. She said no, with her foot. Mrs W took the babe and wrapped it in a blanket which she took from one of the girls . . . the babe felt the warmth and feebly cried . . .

Old women bashed to the point of death by white stockmen, girls as young as eight or nine used as little more than sex slaves, an epidemic of venereal disease — all are contained in Watson's daily chronicle of suffering. Of the white men the missionary could only despair: 'What are my feelings at the conduct of these English stock-keepers may be better conceived than described.' The black men, stripped of their traditional authority and status, were reduced to little more than beggars. Their pathetic attempts at appeasing the white men by selling or lending their women served only to further diminish their manhood, and were rewarded with scorn and contempt. As for the women; Watson considered them the most oppressed of all:

> No class of human beings on the earth can possibly be in a more wretched and pitiable condition than the aboriginal females of New Holland; compelled to look out for food for themselves, and sometimes for the men, and in their journeyings forced to carry many of his weapons; and it may be added, sometimes compelled to yield to the brutal desires of the white men against their will.

On 10 March 1834, Rachael came again to the mission house with King Bobby and two other women. It was two years since she had killed her child to the white man Kelley, and she had another half-caste baby with her, described as 'literally covered with that most loathsome of all diseases', presumably syphilis. Reverend William Watson wrote only, 'We could not prevail on them to stop here.'

I travelled to that same mission where Rachael and her doomed child lived out their lives. Today their descendants still live along the riverbank where William Watson staked out his Christian refuge. It's here I come face to face with my people's tragic legacy. To understand my family — or myself — I need to know our story. So many of the seeds of the Aboriginal malaise of today can be seen to have been sown in the earliest attempts by missionaries to save the blacks. The crippling welfare dependency began with the distribution of rations. The missionaries used food as a means to lure blacks to their settlements. The people quickly realised they would be fed if they attended prayers. This quiet acquiescence masked the blacks' real motives; not to save their souls but to literally save their lives by filling their stomachs. The first signs of the dilution of the Aboriginal bloodline appeared as white settlers used missions as hunting grounds for black women, the mixed blood offspring consigned to an early death or to live as objects of ridicule, rejected by their white fathers.

Similarly, the first signs of black intransigence, or contempt for white authority, began to surface as people wandered on and off the missions at will. By 1838 the mission at Wellington often sheltered as few as six people. And the missionaries themselves, the white saviours of the blacks, were often left dispirited, broken by the lack of compassion from white society and the passive resistance of the Aborigines.

As the whites set about violently disposessing blacks of their land, so too did they turn their minds to the question of what to do with the remnants of the tribes they'd sought to destroy. Australia's selective amnesia about the events of the past was not so much in evidence in the early years of the nineteenth century. In 1814 Governor Lachlan Macquarie, as he sanctioned violence to subdue the blacks, conceived of a future in which the natives would become labourers and useful members of the lower orders of society. He attempted to settle some of the Aborigines of the Sydney district in a fishing village at Elizabeth Bay, but Governor Brisbane reclaimed the land to establish a lunatic asylum there. Macquarie also established a Native Institution to educate black children at Parramatta. There Aboriginal children would be drilled in the teachings of Christianity as much as the three Rs. This laid the foundation for future efforts at civilising the blacks, by emphasising the need to rid them of their savage instincts.

Debate raged throughout the century as to the merits of European settlement, and the responsibilities of the settlers to the people they had displaced. Already there were hints at a sense of manifest destiny, still echoed by some conservatives today. Henry Reynolds highlights this attitude in his book *Dispossession*, quoting one 'W.B.' in a letter about colonisation published in the *Southern Australian* on 8 May 1839:

> Let us therefore hear no more about the right or justice of our proceedings in this repect; or let every sincere objector on this ground prove his sincerity, by at once leaving the country which he thinks he has unjustly taken from another.

By 8 May 1880 a correspondent calling himself 'Never-Never' was more brutally blunt in a letter to the *Queenslander*:

> Is there room for both of us here? No. Then the sooner the weaker is wiped out the better, as we may save some valuable lives in the process.

But compassion stirred in the hearts of others. England kept a close eye on the treatment of indigenous people in its colonies, and in 1836 the House of Commons called for evidence about the treatment of natives in New South Wales and Van Diemen's Land. The testimony made damning reading. In his submission, Archdeacon Broughton of New South Wales concluded:

> They [Aborigines] are in a state which I consider one of extreme degradation and ignorance; they are in fact in a situation much inferior to what I suppose them to have been before they had any communication with Europe.

Broughton described the European settlers as evil, and as perpetrating evil on the blacks. He believed the Aborigines were doomed 'within a very limited period, those who are very much in contact with Europeans will be utterly extinct'. The evidence before the inquiry showed an enlightenment in some quarters and an understanding of preserving Aboriginal customs that would largely vanish by the turn of the century. The colony's Attorney-General, Saxe Bannister, argued that the law was already being used to suppress the blacks:

> So in New South Wales thirty years ago there were atrocious murders of some of the Aborigines; the murderers were tried and there was no doubt of their guilt, but the governor at the time thought it his duty to suspend execution. Now, if it had been the case of white people, execution would have followed immediately.

Bannister argued for Aboriginal interpreters to be used in court. Laws, he said, should be tailored to suit the circumstances and culture of the blacks. Others recognised that the land had been taken from the blacks, illegally and by force, and that a treaty was necessary, just as it had been in parts of North America and New Zealand. But all agreed on one thing, that the only salvation for the Aborigines resided in Christianity. Reverend John Beecham said, 'I regard Christianity as the parent of civilisation, and am persuaded that true civilisation cannot be produced without it.' But the most impassioned template for missionaries was articulated by Archdeacon Broughton:

> As through the tender mercy of our God, the dayspring from on high has visited us, we are solemnly engaged to impart to them glorious beams of gospel truth, to guide their feet in the way of peace.

One who was caught up in those 'beams of gospel truth' was the Reverend William Watson, the man who chronicled Rachael's struggle for survival. A tough-minded teacher from Yorkshire, Watson, like most missionaries, saw in himself the nation's conscience, and viewed the civilising of the blacks as a means for atoning for the brutality of European settlement. 'How large a debt do Britons owe these Aboriginal natives . . . for the physical and moral injuries inflicted by their fellow countrymen,' he said. In 1832 Watson, along with the Reverend Johann Handt, had established the first mission on Wiradjuri land in the Wellington Valley. But Watson and Handt quickly fell out, and Handt was replaced by another German, James Gunther. Gunther, too, quarrelled with Watson; he was offended by the Englishman's coarse language, particularly his swearing during sermons. Gunther was also concerned about Watson's obsession with Aboriginal children. In a chilling portent of government policy, Watson used police to seize children from their parents. Gunther claimed that the women called Watson an eagle-hawk and gave the missionaries the name of kidnappers.

By 1843 the mission had been closed in despair. Its ten years of operation could only be judged a failure. The blacks had been easy victims for white brutality, the women abused and the men degraded. And Christianity, rather than bringing civilisation, had carried with it an inevitable culture clash. As Kennelm Burridge in *Aborigines and Christianity* notes: 'Wherever or whenever Christianity is or has been embraced it rejects parts of a given culture, changes or usages.'

The anthropologist Dr A.P. Elkin wrote: 'the desecration or destruction of the secret life [of the Aborigines] is not the way to success, but is rather the way to cause social disintegration'. What's more, the missionaries seemed unaware of the irony of trying to spread the gospel of love and forgiveness to a people who had been hunted and shot. The commandment 'Thou shalt not steal' must have confused a people who'd seen their land snatched from them. In *Settlers and Convicts*, published in the 1840s, Alexander Harris scoffs at white attempts to preach to blacks, and in a mocking tone imagines the Aborigines' response:

> You who tie one another up and flog one another to within an inch of life for some little hasty word; you, who deprive me of my hunting grounds . . . you a people divided into two classes . . . the tyrant and the slave . . . YOU convert ME, preposterous!

On 26 August 1862, a young man in the Victorian town of Ballarat pledged to devote his life to God. Filled with the joy of the Holy Spirit he couldn't have known then that his commitment to Christ would have profound and sometimes tragic consequences — for himself, and ultimately for my family. During the oppressively hot summer of 1882–83, on a mission he'd named Warrangesda, or Camp of Mercy, on the banks of the Murrumbidgee River, John Brown Gribble would go slowly insane. The daily entries in his diary would reveal a man tortured by his lack of faith and tormented by lust. Around him, the Wiradjuri people he tried to save fell into a state of depravity, victims of white abuse. In the end the blacks themselves would reject their saviour.

John Brown Gribble was born on 1 September 1847 in Cornwall, England. His family moved to the colonies when he was only nine months old. Here he would have his real 'birth', a spiritual awakening with the very people he would one day pledge his life to protect. When John was only a boy he wandered from his family and was lost. A group of Aborigines found him and took him in, caring for the boy until he was reunited with his parents. One can only wonder at what may have taken place, what stirrings were placed in his soul during his time with the blacks, but as a young man his pity for the Aborigines would grow and he would later declare himself 'the friend of the blackfellow'.

Gribble read his Bible with a passion. While working as a miner he would take it into the dark depths to read by candlelight. A man of commitment and zeal, his determination and perhaps his foolhardiness were glimpsed during a curious run-in with the bushranger Ned Kelly. John Gribble was a travelling parson in the Victorian goldfields in 1879 when the Kelly Gang made its historic raid on the township of Jerilderie. The young parson was among those rounded up, and Kelly's partner in crime, Steve Hart, took Gribble's watch. Gribble later fronted Ned himself, and standing eyeball to eyeball demanded his watch back. Gribble's bold show of courage worked; Kelly retrieved the watch and, handing it to the parson, sent him on his way.

Gribble's preaching round allowed him to see first-hand the suffering of Aboriginal people. He recorded his distress and horror in a book published in 1884, *Black But Comely*:

> I unexpectedly came into contact with the blacks. I found them in a condition most shocking to contemplate. I visited their camps! I entered their wretched bark and bough gunyas. I went from place to place, and everywhere I met with the same wretchedness and woe.

Gribble wrote about discovering a bundle of dirty rags under some bushes, and finding it contained a little girl: 'How my heart sickened, and my blood warmed!' He blamed the suffering on the 'professedly Christian white man!' Later that night the parson threw himself upon his knees and wept before God: 'O Lord, show me Thy way; teach me Thy path; tell me what to do for these perishing Aborigines.' When Gribble rose to his feet he knew what he must do; from that moment he became a missionary.

Gribble became so obsessed with the welfare of Aborigines that the locals in Jerilderie believed that 'Parson Gribble had developed "blacks on the brain".' In 1880 he realised his dream of a mission station where blacks could find a haven from the brutality of the Australian frontier. The site of Warrangesda, near the small town of Darlington Point on the Murrumbidgee, was chosen by Gribble and his friend, Daniel Mathews, who'd already established the Maloga mission school. Gribble had left Jerilderie with a handful of Aborigines, and roamed the countryside collecting others, often by force. Darlington Point he described as the 'very focus of iniquity', and the blacks were not always keen to see him:

> I was stopping in front of a store when a black woman came forward reeling under the influence of drink given her by white men. She took up a large stick as soon as she saw me and threw the stick at me.

Gribble's aim, above all else, was to Christianise the blacks; prayer, faith and hope, he said, were as essential as reading, writing and arithmetic. But like many before him, Gribble experienced resistance from the white locals. Within a few months of opening Warrangesda, he was shut down by the Lands Department, but the courage he showed in the face of the Kelly Gang allowed him to prevail and soon he was operating again, building a schoolhouse, a store and huts for the blacks.

Within only two years, however, the strain had begun to show and Gribble was unravelling; in his own words his mind was becoming 'unhinged'. The full extent of his despair is writ large in the pages of his diary.

3 January 1882 Working with the black men, feeling spiritually very low. I allow little things to trouble me too much.

4 January 1882 I am ashamed of my bitterness of faith and zeal. I do earnestly desire to live a life of real faith in God. Without faith it is impossible to please him.

5 January 1882 This evening I feel very weary both in body and mind.

6 January 1882 Quite done up, body and mind wrung out. At such times the devil comes in like a flood and threatens to overwhelm me. Very low spiritually, waves and billows going over my soul.

7 January 1882 Getting very hot again, 104 degrees in the shade. Spiritually in deep gloom. Hardly know what is coming over me. I only cling to Christ's mercy and love, like a drowning man to a fragment of rock.

8 January 1882 Too completely dark and mentally tempest to conduct morning service with the blacks. All I could do was to lie in my bed and sigh over my sins and wish for eternal rest.

Not only was Gribble struggling with self-doubt and a crisis of faith, the stifling heat began to take a toll on him physically. Set against a black society imploding, the soaring temperature meant in every sense that John Brown Gribble had found his personal hell.

8 JANUARY 1882 Very hot, 112 degrees in the shade, the wind has been just like the blast from a furnace.

9 JANUARY 1882 Still very hot, 104 degrees in the shade. Sambo left today because I reproached him for indolence; he is a lazy fellow and can't bear being told of his faults.

10 JANUARY 1882 Working at fever. Terribly hot, 112 degrees in shade, hot wind and clouds of dust.

Like many missionaries, Gribble could not see Aborigines as anything but childlike. He constantly chided them and took away the authority of the men to make decisions for themselves and their families. Warrangesda began to resemble a prison and runaways were chased down. Many of the blacks were ready to rebel.

15 JANUARY 1882 Trying experience last night. Sambo decoyed away his wife and she, Sarah, it seems induced Lena to run away. After prayers they were missed and Mr Bridle and I started in pursuit and tracked them across the river which they crossed in a tiny bark canoe . . . At daybreak Mr Bridle and I returned and I got into the mail coach and continued the pursuit. They had arrived there at sunrise and had gone up the river with the local blacks fishing. Got some breakfast and borrowed a horse and rode after them. Soon overtook them and after some altercation compelled them to return . . . I am

> completely knocked up. Slept well last night. Had to perform a most unthankful task this afternoon, the chastisement of Lena for running away. All but Aggie, her sister, semed to think she well deserved it, but Aggie made a great uproar and tried hard to arouse the whole camp to opposition. She gave me great abuse . . .

Gribble, who had begun with the most admirable intentions, fired by a passion to end Aboriginal suffering, had become himself part of the problem. He'd become prone to the paternalism that has afflicted Aboriginal policy to this day. He was like an overseer who depends on the goodwill of the very people he enslaves.

Gribble's problems, though, were not only with the Aborigines. Whites, too, had begun to sense his desperation and were turning against him.

> 17 January 1882 Received insult and injury from Mr Bridle, which made me very ill. My mind is so critical at the present time that I cannot stand such an experience. My mind lost its balance, I know it did, and Bridle was the cause of it.
>
> 18 January 1882 I have decided to ask the bishop to release me from my position in favour of Mr Bridle, who seems to desire chief position.

Gribble was torn between walking away and persevering. He would many times resign, and then rethink his decision. But he continued to sink further into melancholia. The heat sapped his energy, and his depression grew debilitating. He often went days without food, and sometimes could not stir himself from his bed. On his good days, however, he continued to travel the countryside rounding up blacks to take to Warrangesda.

> 1 February 1882 Rose early. Albert and I sought out and found blacks' camp. Found about thirty men, women and children, all in a sad state of semi-nakedness and hunger. Gave a man some money to buy bread. Talked vividly to all about Warrangesda. Several seemed willing to go, but some of the older ones were very direct in opposing my suggestion . . . I hope to take about a dozen away with me.
>
> 3 February 1882 Took twelve poor waifs and strays from Cootamundra to the mission station.

Among the Aborigines Gribble 'collected' were members of the Gibson, Naden and Foster families. These people would form the core of the Warrangesda community and their blood runs through my veins today.

Gribble continued to grow weaker and more depressed. He wrote of being 'overcome' and 'prostrate'. His diary also reveals a man struggling to control his lust. He despised white men for exploiting black women, and pitied their half-caste offspring. Yet slowly he began to resemble what he so hated. A form of self-flagellation began to characterise his writings, and on his wedding anniversary he made a private confession of his sins.

> 4 February 1882 Fourteen years married to a young amiable lady named M.A.E. Bulmer. Oh what changes since that interesting and solemn event. How much of my unfaithfulness to God and my own dear wife has marked my way since that event. And here I am today in the midst of my poor life work, in the face of mountainous difficulties trying to prosecute it. But I am a poor instrument, an unworthy vessel, a bruised reed.

Gribble continued to struggle for the rest of the year. He never again mentioned his infidelity, but his diary betrayed his fragile grip on sanity. He also hardened his belief that only he knew what was good for the blacks. In 1883 he was determined to start afresh.

> 1 January 1883 My motto for this year shall be, 'Ye are not your own for ye are bought with a price. Therefore glorify God in your body and in your spirit which are God's.'

What quickly emerged was evidence of more black rebellion. Their sometimes passive resistance to Gribble's authority was turning violent, and they refused to heed his messages of Christian morality.

17 February 1883 Discovered that three girls had been guilty of immorality, three of the Namoi men implicated. I held a court with all the men of the place. It was decided to strictly caution the men as it was their first known offence. The girls were imprisoned for three days and three nights. Preached this morning to blacks from 'The wicked shall be turned into hell'. Afternoon, conducted Sunday school.

Aborigines were by then arriving at Warrangesda from all over the state. Gribble had begun the dangerous practice of mixing people from different areas with different beliefs, customs and languages. It was often a recipe for disaster, with black-on-black clashes common, and the community on the verge of self-destruction. Rachel King was among a group of blacks brought to Warrangesda from La Perouse in Sydney. She led her group in open revolt, continually defying Gribble's authority. During a two-day rampage she disrupted the parson's sermons, disturbed a picnic and looted the mission store, taking food and drink. Finally Gribble had to call in the police, but it crushed his spirit and he considered giving up his work.

The men of the mission began to form themselves into political groups agitating for change. The half-caste men were demanding the right to drink alcohol, which Gribble steadfastly refused. The men finally formed a deputation and travelled to Sydney to lodge a complaint with the government. Gribble was losing his grip on the people, and began to enforce harsh penalties for disobedience. These were to have disastrous consequences for one young girl known as Rosie Snowden.

> 25 February 1883 A newly born infant has been discovered in Rosie Snowden's box this morning. She concealed the birth from Monday morning. Fresh troubles. Truly this is a vexatious work. I feel disgusted with the whole thing. Rebels returned from Sydney. They got no encouragement, but were told to quit the mission if they would not obey the rules.
>
> Rosie Snowden taken in charge on concealment of birth. Poor misguided creature. The rebels with their wives left the mission this morning. It really seems as if the place must be broken up. I want to do what is right, but it is hard to do so. Oh Lord, do help us through all these troubles.

By 30 July Rosie Snowden had been tried for concealment of birth and sentenced to three months in prison. Aboriginal resistance to white authority, whether by drinking or giving birth without the mission manager's permission, was a criminal act. The hostile relationship between blacks and the police and Aboriginal over-representation in prisons can be seen to have taken root more than a hundred years ago. If people like poor Rosie Snowden suffered, so too did

Gribble, although by then it could be seen to be a suffering of his own making.

> 12 SEPTEMBER 1883 Body weary and mind depressed. Spiritually in conflict with the powers of darkness. God help me.

Gribble's plea for God's mercy would be answered only in defeat. In 1884 he suffered a complete breakdown and was shipped to England to recover. When he returned, nothing had changed. Finally he could take no more, and in 1885 left the mission he founded. He left it a broken man, a man who'd stared into the abyss and saw only inevitable destruction for the people he'd once hoped to save.

But Gribble's passion for the Aborigines returned and he moved to Western Australia, where the pattern was to be repeated. He tried to highlight the miserable plight of blacks in the west and was repaid with violence from the whites. Ultimately he left there too, broken and defeated. His son, Ernest, refused to be deterred and followed in his father's footsteps, also becoming a missionary.

Gribble had gone from the Wiradjuri but the course of my people was unalterably set. Other missions had sprung up where the remnants of the Wiradjuri were left to face what whites believed would be their rapid extinction. In some cases that almost proved true.

Mandagery Creek now runs gently through the quiet little town of Eugowra, but once its waters ran red with blood as my people fought a battle of almost complete annihilation, not with the whites but with each other. The Mandagery Creek massacre was never recorded in the history books, but lived on in the memories and oral traditions of both whites and blacks. Local historian Robert Ellis wrote of the story after talking to old Jim Goolagong from Condobolin:

> The natives of the area were experiencing the kind of complete tribal breakdown which inevitably followed white settlement. One day the evident despair and distrust finally came to a head and the Aboriginal men, women and children began fighting among themselves. When the awesome battle came to an end almost every man, woman and child was either dead or dying. Some lay battered on the ground and others had actually climbed into the branches of high trees to die.

Violence came to characterise much of mission life. The resistance shown by some of the Warrangesda blacks to Gribble's rule faded into an uneasy accommodation, a reluctant acquiescence to their subjugation. Warrangesda and other missions, rather than being hotbeds of discontent, instead, for many, became simply home.

The next wave of the Aboriginal political struggle would be plotted from the huts at Warrangesda and its neighbouring mission, Cummeragunja, but this would not be a campaign for the recognition of the sovereignty that Wiindhuraydhine and others had fought for. Rather it would be a fight for citizenship and equality with the whites. Though railing against racism, the blacks showed signs of a deepening acceptance of paternalism. By campaigning to enjoy the same rights as whites, the Aboriginal leadership was inherently recognising the legitimacy of white society. We'd failed to transform into a society conscious of itself; we were fashioning ourselves not after our own image but that of the whites.

In 1896 on Warrangesda mission, a baby girl was born to Frank Foster and Lydia Naden. Florence Foster would become affectionately known as 'Nanny Cot', and would grow to be the matriarch of a large black clan. Nanny would raise her children, some of her grandchildren and even great-grandchildren. Sadly, in her more than eighty years she would see many of her offspring die before her. As a young woman Cot Foster married Wilfred Johnson and moved to Condobolin, where she lived alongside the few remaining survivors of the bloody Mandagery Creek massacre. Nanny Cot was my great-grandmother.

7

Strangers in Their Land

Only the successful are remembered . . .
The blind alleys, the lost causes and the losers themselves are forgotten.
E.P. THOMPSON,
THE MAKING OF THE ENGLISH WORKING CLASS

Frank Foster was what turn-of-the-century whites liked to call, with no hint of affection, a cheeky black bastard. He skipped through the pages of history with an impish grin, humping his swag and moving from mission to mission as the law closed in around him. Frank aspired to be like the white men he saw around the blacks' camps, yet at the same time he challenged white authority, ensuring he would never be anything other than what he was born — a blackfella.

There's no-one alive today who can tell me about Frank Foster; no-one who remembers what he looked like, how he spoke, how he dressed, what he laughed at or what he liked to eat. There's no-one who can tell me whether he was a good man or bad, no-one who can say whether he retained his dignity or allowed the systematic white abuse to destroy him. There's no photograph for me to look at to see if I resemble this man who was my great-great-grandfather.

For all that's missing, I feel as though I know Frank Foster as well as if he were sitting here with me now. His life is writ large in the official records of the day; a man whose every move was monitored by the managers of the Aboriginal reserves he lived on, whose ambition would be frustrated because his black skin made him, in the eyes of many Australians, less than human — at best an object of pity, at worst not fit for white society. Grandfather Frank's life was lived out in the brutal years before and after the New South Wales *Aborigines Protection Act* came into effect in 1909. Like thousands of his fellow countrymen, Frank had no control over where he could live, whether he could stay with his family, where he could work and whether he could share a drink with his mates. The dragnet of these restrictive laws would forever close in around him, forcing on him the life of an outlaw, moved from reserve to reserve, never really finding a place to call home.

Frank Foster was born at Kiama on the New South Wales south coast on 1 January 1872. His sister Bella would be born two years later and another sister,

Bessie, in 1879. Frank was born into a rapidly changing society; not yet a hundred years had passed since the English claimed this continent for their new colony, yet Frank carried the white man's blood and his name. By the 1870s the traditions of Frank's forefathers were irretrievably shattered. Aboriginal society was in a process of mutation. For the most part, this was not gradual, evolutionary change; rather it was the type of revolutionary transformation experienced by pre-modern societies the world over as they were superseded by a more advanced technology. The old Aboriginal culture was quickly supplanted and those who survived the initial impact of dispossession were fashioning a world based not only on their shared history and memory of their culture, but shaped by the powerful new forces of exclusion from white society.

White paternalism had one aim: to make the black people white. For paternalism to work there needs to be a subordinate, someone who is prepared to accept their suffering as legitimate: 'Yes, boss; anything you say, boss; three bags full, boss.' Survival doesn't honour pride. Frank Foster's options were limited to a slow death as a blackfella or a bare existence on the bottom rung of white society.

It's a mistake even to think of Grandfather Frank as a blackfella. By the time he was born there was little to inherit from his Aboriginal forebears: the bora grounds, where he would have become a man, had vanished into the dust; the hunters were beggars; and the young women who would have been promised to him were riddled with disease, or pregnant to a white man, or both. His fate was the cruel misery of someone trying to be what they're not. The cruellest cut of all was that in everything he had little or no choice.

One of the factors reshaping the society Frank Foster was born into was the anthropological concept of social Darwinism, reflected in notions of the survival of the fittest and the white man's burden. These in turn promoted policies of assimilation and protection, as Aboriginal historian Gordon Briscoe has noted: 'The anthropologists were the ideologues of modern protectionist policies that directly affected race relations in Australia.'

The anthropologists — and the missionaries — sought vindication for their policies in the rapidly changing Aboriginal demography. The Aboriginal population was being transformed, physically as well as socially. As the whites exterminated the blacks and excluded the remnants from the post-frontier society, they were, at the same time, leaving a new legacy in the coffee-coloured faces of part-Aboriginal children. By 1901 the number of Aborigines in New South Wales had plunged to a little over 8000 from around 40 000 in 1788. By the time of my birth in 1963 the population had recovered to about 14 000, the number swollen by the rise of the so-called half-castes.

In 1882, ten years after Frank Foster's birth, the Aborigines Protection Board was established to aid the efforts of missionaries in training half-castes to become useful members of society. The full bloods were expected to die out, and the missionaries saw it as their role to protect the mixed bloods. Australian settlers had exercised their power from behind the barrel of a gun and they knew that their violence needed the legitimacy of the law.

This is the matrix through which the young Frank Foster would view the world. As Frank grew to adolesence, the preacher John Brown Gribble, of Warrangesda fame, was already honouring his pledge to God to work for the salvation of Aboriginal people. Gribble had been inspired by the work of another missionary, Daniel Mathews, who had established the Maloga mission school. Mathews had been 'touched with deepest sorrow' for the Aborigines' plight and determined to 'redeem their helpless little ones'. Mathews was a strict Wesleyan Methodist, the type who had taken a foothold in Britain after the industrial revolution. This was a denomination that made a virtue of suffering; in Britain its impact was greatest among the industrial working class and its prescription for social control would fit equally the Australian frontier. Historian E.P. Thompson described Methodism as:

> . . . the consolidation of a new bureaucracy of ministers who regarded it as their duty to manipulate the submissiveness of their followers and to discipline all deviant growths within the church which could give offence to authority.

Mathews and his disciple Gribble saw their mission as not only to save and educate the blacks, but more importantly to teach them the gospel. Faith and prayer were as important as reading and writing.

In 1881 Frank and his sisters were rounded up as the missionaries cast their net wide throughout the state to find suitable candidates for training. Of the Foster children's parents, my great-great-great-grandparents, I know nothing. That part of my family tree which had existed uninterrupted for thousands of generations was forever severed as little Frank, Bella and Bessie were taken away, never to see their mother and father again. The children found themselves in the Riverina amongst strangers, people who did not share what was left of their traditions or their language. This was a brutal time.

Frank Foster remained at Maloga for ten years, until he and his sisters were transferred to the mission at Cummeragunja on the New South Wales side of the Murray River. Frank had grown into a cheeky young man with enough intelligence to fancy himself as the next schoolteacher on the mission. This was a bold move, and far outstripped the meagre ambition Mathews had in mind for young Frank when he brought him from Kiama to Maloga. Whatever Frank's qualifications or aspirations, the Aborigines Protection Board was determined no blackfella would become anything as lofty as a teacher. On 13 October 1892, the board considered the results of an inquiry into Frank's character and found him lacking. Frank had been appointed to train in the teaching position, but any hopes he may have had of filling the role permanently would be cruelly dashed. The Protection Board concluded coldly: '. . . the board consider it in the last degree inadvisable to retain Foster in the position to which the association had appointed him.'

Grandfather Frank lived at Cummeragunja for another two and a half frustrating years. He remained under the watchful eye of the mission manager, now suspicious of the young man's ambition and audacity. Finally he was moved to the Warrangesda mission at Darlington Point, which had been established by the ill-fated Gribble in 1880. As described in Chapter 6, Gribble had plunged into madness as the blacks rebelled against his authority and the local whites used his mission to run grog and prey on black women who were easy targets for sexual abuse. By the time Frank Foster arrived in 1895, Gribble had long since moved on; his legacy lived on, though, in a generation of blacks dependent on the mission as the only place they had ever called home.

Frank married a Warrangesda woman, Lydia Naden, whose family had been among the first Aborigines Gribble rounded up and moved onto the mission. Like her husband, Lydia was a half-caste, her Aboriginal blood mixed with Scottish and Maori genes. The mission was seemingly on track in its aim to smooth the dying pillow of the full-bloods. In July 1891 there were forty-three full-bloods and forty-six half-castes; a mission census taken in September of that year showed a population of 180, but the people were soon ravaged by an epidemic of typhoid. By 1902 the full-bloods on the mission numbered thirty-four and the half-castes eighty. The mission had struggled under a succession of ineffective managers who tried to introduce farming and run livestock. The blacks, though, were quickly adapting to some aspects of mission life, embracing religion and that most British of sports, cricket. The Aborigines were keen sportsmen and the mission cricket team had a strong reputation throughout the district. Frank Foster, though, was batting from the losing end. The restrictive laws and meddling of the mission managers meant life was destined never to run smooth.

On 3 June 1896 Frank Foster became a father. Lydia had given birth to a little girl they named Florence — my great-grandmother, Nanny Cot. The responsibility of a wife and child may have eased Frank's restlessness and despair after a lifetime at the whim of the Aborigines Protection Board. But this was not to be a new beginning; within a few short years the Foster family was split up when the manager of Warrangesda ordered Frank be expelled from the mission for defying his authority. Frank spent fifteen months in limbo, homeless and living on the fringes of town. Possibly he stayed close to Warrangesda, perhaps sneaking in at night to visit his family.

Finally he applied to the Protection Board to be allowed to rejoin his sisters at Cummeragunja; the board agreed on the basis of a six-month probation, a condition Frank was unwilling to accept. How Frank lived for the next few years remains a mystery as he vanishes from the official records. Did he have another family? Did he sink into a depression, drinking and gambling? There is no indication he ever made it home to Warrangesda, ever reunited with Lydia and baby Florence. Family folklore says he wandered the countryside, spending some time in jail.

When Frank resurfaces in the official records he was back in the land of his birth on the New South Wales south coast. By 1916 he was living at the Roseby Park Aboriginal settlement near Nowra, but yet again he ran foul of authority. By that time the *Aborigines Protection Act* of 1909 was in place, fixing in legislation the restrictive practices that Frank had endured all of his life. On 12 October 1916 the Protection Board made its final entry in the life of my great-great-grandfather: 'Expulsion of half-caste Frank Foster from Roseby Park Aboriginal Station for defiance of the board's authority, gambling, etc.'

So Frank Foster was written out of the pages of history and in time wiped even from the memory of my family. Born to the remnants of the tribes that scattered along the south coast of the state, he was destined to wander the last of his days in obscurity. Grandfather Frank's life was never his own: he was snatched from his parents to be trained to one day enter white society, but when a flash of intelligence and a streak of impudence allowed him to aspire to something better, to be a schoolteacher, the Protection

Board snatched it from his grasp. When he married and had a family, the board made sure he would never make a home. His story speaks to me today as sure as his blood runs through my veins. Frank lived a life we would all live to varying degrees: no longer just black but never to be white; unable to reach back to the world from which he came, unable to reach out to the world from which he was excluded. My great-great-grandfather died as he had lived — in the shadows of the new Australian nation after a lifetime searching for, but never finding, the light of its grace.

Frank Foster's story may appear remarkable — it isn't. The same tale of torment and loneliness was played out among men and women on any number of the Aboriginal reserves scattered across New South Wales. My tracks led me back to places with names like Cummeragunja, Warrangesda, Maloga and Bulgandramine; places that have vanished from the landscape but remain still in the memories of the families who forged this new Aboriginal society. Bulgandramine is a white man's word; the Wiradjuri people knew it as Bulkandhuraymine, it meant 'people having boomerangs'. The mission along the banks of the Bogan River near the small mid-western town of Peak Hill has been empty for more than sixty years. Once, though, Bulgandramine was home to dozens of families: the Dargins, Powells, Grays, Reads and Governors. They were known as the mudlarks, and the old people who can still recall the mission remember a happy time. Rita Keed has compiled many of their stories in *Memories of Bulgandramine Mission*.

> Even through the bad times and sad times the people showed courage and strength of character. Government rules and regulations restricted their way of life but this did not dampen their happy and caring nature.

Among the names recalled from the old mission days is Bill Grant, my great-grandfather; he was known to all simply as 'the storyteller'.

I draw comfort from where I stand now at the site of the old mission. I never lived here, yet this land carries so much of my family's story. I watched the sunrise this morning over the top of the trees along the riverbank. It lit up the earth and its rays warmed my body; just as it had done a hundred years ago when my great-grandfather Bill made his home here. All around me is silence now, but slowly I'm learning to hear again, to unblock the white noise of the city from my head. My ears open to the sounds of the world turning: the flutter of the birds in the trees, the far-off squawking of the crows, and the wind rustling through the leaves. This land, my land, was shaking itself from its sleep; another day gently marking the turning of time, gathering up its stories, its secrets, and holding them close.

Once this place rang with the sounds of life. As I stare into the river I can see the little children ducking and diving, their mothers dragging the water into their tin buckets. On this same morning, in another time, the air would have filled with the smoke from the camp fires. Hot tea, johnnycakes (the blackfellas' damper), kangaroo in a bit of onion and gravy would have filled their stomachs. But the idyllic picture is tempered with a much more harsh reality. Here were a dislocated people, a people involved, in every sense, in a life and death struggle. The missionaries carried tales of sickness and sorrow in monthly reports in the magazine *Our A.I.M.*, published by the Aborigines Inland Mission. In June 1919 missionary Miss Taylor wrote:

> . . . sickness has come amongst our people. We are glad to have little Frankie with us again after a severe attack of pneumonia. One of our old men is still in hospital with pleurisy, and yesterday a mother took her baby in — bronchitis and pneumonia is the trouble.

In 1915 Bill Grant and Catherine Ryan had a baby daughter, Eunice. You remember Bill, my link to the brutality of the Australian frontier. I think of him now as the first Australian in my family, someone who carried both black and white within him in equal measure and whose life was lived in the greyness between the two. Bill had eleven children to his first wife, Margaret Brien; Catherine also had a large family, and between them Bill and Catherine had another four children, including my grandfather, Cec. Little Eunice had the misfortune to be born to elderly parents, and onto a mission where her life would be ruled by the 1909 *Aborigines Protection Act*. Along with its restrictions on the Aborigines' liberty, the Act had as its stated aim the removal of half-caste children from the reserves. The New South Wales Aborigines Protection Board's power over children was bolstered by the *Neglected Children and Juvenile Offenders Act* 1905. This law and its amendment in 1915 gave the board power to 'remove such child to such control and care as it thinks best'. As John Chesterman and Brian Galligan point out in *Citizens Without Rights*: 'Under the board's dispersal policy, over 1500 Aboriginal children were separated from their families between 1912 and 1938.'

On a June day in 1927 my great-aunt Eunice Grant became one of those statistics. Like Frank Foster's, Aunty Eunice's life would be one lived under the eye of the law, her every move controlled by the oppressive *Aborigines Protection Act*.

As I look at an old black and white photo of the young Aboriginal girls taken from their families, I see far more than a mere reading of the law or of the missionaries' reports could ever convey. The girls are lined up outside the welfare home at Cootamundra, a mixture of ages, sizes and skin tones. Twelve-year-old Eunice Grant is in the middle, a tiny girl with a grim mouth and eyes staring into space. I recognise that look;

it's the same one I see today on the face of my Aunty Elaine, Eunice's daughter. There's a wistfulness there, a loneliness and an unspoken plea to be loved. Aunty Elaine never knew her mother; Eunice died with her baby in her arms. Maybe that's the connection I see — of love lost, never to be regained. Elaine was raised by my grandparents, her uncle and aunty; that makes her my dad's sister. I know she wonders sometimes if she really belongs, but I love you Aunty, and I love the memory of your mum too.

One or two girls in the photo are trying to force a smile; the rest simply don't bother. In most cases these girls would never see their parents again; some may never have seen any of their family again. Their destiny would be a life of servitude as maids, housekeepers and nannies for wealthy squatter families. Some would grow to be ashamed of their Aboriginal heritage, their self-hatred often passed on to their children and the generation after that. None of the girls in the photo would emerge unscathed. They would become part of what would later popularly be known as the stolen generation. Now we pick over their misery, reducing the fact of their lives to an argument. In their tears others see dollar signs and convince themselves that their memories can be laid to rest in the judgments of courtrooms. Sometimes I want to scream to leave them alone; but am I so different? I draw succour for my soul from their misery, I wear their suffering like a badge — or better still a medal of war — and bludgeon whites with my self-righteousness.

Stolen generation? That's an argument for white Australia. White historians exaggerate numbers then revise them. Governments hold inquiries, call it genocide, then change their minds. Journalists pick apart individual lives, seize on semantics and call us liars. Some pull it apart like a historical house of cards; others, just as delicately, piece it together. Some deny outright there was a stolen generation at all. All I know is there are gaping holes in our photo albums, names we'll never put faces to.

Was Aunty Eunice stolen? Does it matter? A life can't be reduced to a catchy slogan. If she wasn't stolen, simply removed, does that make her pain, her family's pain, any less real? To the missionaries and the reserve manager, Eunice Grant was a neglected little black girl, living in poverty, surrounded by disease and in need of saving. In her they saw not blackness but the promise of whiteness. In her father's eyes, Eunice was just his dear little daughter.

The report of the Aborigines Protection Board reads so coldly, so matter-of-factly. Aunty Eunice is known as case number 658; the report lists her name, her age and place of birth. Under the heading 'Reason for board assuming control of child' it reads: 'Being neglected. No fixed place of abode and on the report and recommendation of the manager of the Aboriginal Station, Cowra.'

Her father is listed as William Grant, labourer, Goolagong. Eunice's mother is listed as deceased; her other relatives are noted, incorrectly, as one brother and one sister. Eunice in fact had been living with her sister Emma Merritt and Emma's husband, Bill, on Bulgandramine. On 18 June 1927 she entered the Cootamundra Girls Home; three years later Eunice was transferred to the Angledool Aboriginal Station in the far west of the state. On 9 October 1930 Eunice Grant, aged fifteen, was sent into service for Mrs L.J. Sevil at Colleymugga station, Angledool. On 16 April 1935 Eunice was back with her father, Bill, on the Cowra Aboriginal Station. These are the bare facts of Eunice Grant's early life; they don't tell of the heartbreaking sadness of a little girl taken from her family, of her struggle to find a way back home, nor the hardness of a life that would end tragically young.

What a contrast it is to look at Eunice Grant's life and the lives of her white cousins on the vast Grant properties around Canowindra. A hundred years earlier Wongamar had met the white Irish convict John Grant; in time their blood would become one, yet their offspring would be cruelly separated by the colour of their skins. Denied his heritage, Bill Grant, his mother, Mary Ann, and his brothers and sisters lived as flotsam and jetsam on the sea of colonial Australian history. The Wiradjuri language had fallen silent, the bullroarer could no longer be heard summoning the young boys to become men, the footprints of the tribal dancers vanished into the earth. Bill Grant and his children were expected to emerge as white when their dark skin and the bigotry of the Australian frontier told them otherwise.

While Bill raised his family on Bulgandramine, his cousin John Grant junior was tending the Grant holdings of Merriganowry and Grantwood. Grandfather Bill had been born and raised in the shadow of the big house while his mother worked for those she was related to by blood. Bill would return on and off to work on Grantwood. While the black Grants lived under the 'Act' in tin humpies and tents, surrounded by death and disease, the white Grants enjoyed a life of privilege — the inheritance of old John, who'd died the wealthiest Irish Catholic in the colony. John Grant junior's diary reveals days working the land, playing social cricket, horse riding and long, sumptuous Sunday dinners. A typical diary entry of Sunday, 17 September 1905 reads:

> I rode over to Belabula to see my father — I left Grantville at a quarter past nine, got to Belabula at 12 — had dinner with father, mother, and sister Mary . . . I wonder will we ever have Sunday dinner together at Belabula again. That night I slept in my old bedroom — and what memories of the past life — long ago — came over me.

Eunice Grant's memories I doubt would have been so sweet.

Aunty Eunice eventually found a home on the Condobolin mission alongside her brother, my grandfather, Cec Grant, and his wife, Josephine Johnson. This was the late 1930s and early 1940s, the period of dispersal and assimilation, when people could be classified and declassified Aboriginal depending on the whim of the mission manager. The Condobolin mission is remembered as a particularly harsh place, where men would be led through the streets chained together, where Alsatian dogs would be set loose on anyone breaking the mission law.

Historian Charles Rowley wrote about people like Eunice and Bill Grant in his book *Outcasts in White Australia*. Years of research left Rowley with one simple, heartbreaking conclusion:

> Those part-Aborigines who inherited only what the whites left for the blacks have remained ever since at the mercy of what seem arbitrary decisions. The only escape has been by fading away out of part-Aboriginal society.

Aunty Eunice, though, was determined to cling to her people, to the only way of life in which she could ever feel comfortable. But her tenacity came at a price: the cost of her liberty. After being removed from her family and sent to work for white squatters in a far-off part of the state, she found that even on the Condobolin mission, amongst her family, she couldn't escape the restrictive policies of the Aborigines Welfare Board, which had inherited responsibility for the reserves from the former Protection Board. Eunice Grant had been married to half-caste Lindsay Sloane, but that relationship had ended and she was living with a man named Jacky Johnson, also known by his tribal name Moolbong.

Her relationship was in defiance of the policy of breeding out Aboriginal blood. Eunice was designated a half-caste, and it was hoped after her training that she would seek to find a place on the fringes of white society, perhaps marry a white man and have quarter-caste children. Living with Moolbong, a full-blood, meant her children would get blacker not whiter. On 27 June 1944 Eunice Sloane (nee Grant) had to apply to the Welfare Board for permission to live with her de facto husband on the Condobolin reserve, permission to live with a man she loved in the only home she'd ever known. Within a few years Eunice, the daughter of Bill Grant and Catherine Ryan from Bulgandramine mission, great-granddaughter of the richest Catholic squatter in the colonies, John Grant, was dead. She left behind six little children, including my Aunty Elaine, the youngest. They were left with nothing but the comfort that maybe in death Aunty Eunice found a freedom she'd never known in life.

The experiences of Grandfather Frank and Aunty Eunice are the scars that will not heal among my people. They were sacrificed to Australia's whiteness. In the face of their pain, Australians would build a myth of tolerance and egalitarianism. Sometimes even I'm guilty of rationalising the past, justifying my family's torment as merely the unhappy by-product of a less enlightened time. Surely Australians today should not be held responsible for history? Surely on the balance sheet of this nation's account there is more in credit than debit? I disgrace their memory to even think like that. A nation is not divided into columns; it is the sum of all of its parts, with none having greater weight than the other.

The pain and suffering of people like Frank and Eunice have formed the bedrock of modern Aboriginal political claims of injustice. How do we convince you that our tears are real, when all you see are the tears of strangers — nothing but water. To find an excuse in the benefit of hindsight is to say that there was a time when we were less than human. Were people really that callous? What did they see when they looked upon the sad faces of children taken from their parents? The best we could hope for was a missionary's pity; and pity is not compassion.

Aborigines were easy prey. Frank Foster and Eunice Grant found themselves caught in a moment of history when paternalism, ignorance and outright racism clashed with a culture undergoing rapid change. We'd survived isolation for tens of thousands of years, but we could not survive discovery. We had no agriculture, no domestic animals, no money, no factories, cities or towns; we had nothing the whites could call civilisation. The whites came here with the microscope, telescope, barometer, clock and steam engine; yet for all their technology they would soon show they lacked the basic unit of humanity: empathy. They could not look — they would not allow themselves to look — into our eyes and see themselves.

The whites preached from their Bible; they told us the way to civilisation was through their Christian God. But they read their scripture selectively. They broke their own commandments: 'Thou shalt not steal'; 'Thou shalt not murder'; 'Thou shalt not commit adultery'; then they told us we must have no other gods before theirs. In spite of it all, we believed them.

8

Blessed are the Peacemakers

If dere ain't a heaven, what's coloured folks got to look forward to . . .
ANNE BELL, SLAVE

I saw my Uncle Frank cry today. I've never seen him cry before, but I suppose you're allowed to when you bury your brother. We all sang 'The Old Rugged Cross'; blackfellas always sing that at funerals, gentle songs in soft voices. Funerals bring us together, they call us home, not just to say goodbye, but to remind us where we belong, or in my case where I don't. I hadn't been home to Griffith since we buried my grandmother. Uncle Frank was there that day as well, the Aboriginal pastor leading the service to send his aunty on to the promised land. We sang 'The Old Rugged Cross' that day too. My dad cried, and I cried as I helped my brothers and my cousins lower our nan's coffin into the ground.

On a hill far away, stood an old rugged cross,
a symbol of suffering and shame . . .
and I'll cherish that old rugged cross
'til my trophies at last I lay down.
I will cling to the old rugged cross
and exchange it some day for a crown.

'Look for a man's wealth, that's where his heart is'; the Bible tells us that. Laurie Johnson's wealth was in his laughter and his kindness, and in his soul — the soul of an Aboriginal man who loved his people. I've been around so-called rich people of whom you couldn't say the same. Laurie was only fifty, far too young to die, yet in blackfella terms he was already an old man. Some would say the grog killed him, but that tells only part of the story. Laurie Johnson lived and died as a Koori; he called himself, proudly, a Wiradjuri. Yet Laurie, like all of us there to pay our respects, had the blood of white people in his veins and lived much of his life away from Wiradjuri country. His black forebears had long since given up the old ways and stopped speaking in their own tongue. Laurie had lived his life caught between sin and redemption, now he was given a Christian burial.

There's James. For a time, he was my best friend at school; now I have to look twice to recognise him. He's changed, James. Thirty-seven years doesn't look like this; it shouldn't anyway. How do we compare ourselves? How do I measure my years against his? I realise now we only truly connect at some time in the past; a past I return to each fleeting visit back home. It's a past James measures in years, but I measure in distance. It's a past I remember; it's a past he can't escape. This is Auden's 'Crossroads': 'The friends that met her and embraced, were gone; each to his own mistake.'

Luck. Yeah, that's it: luck. Some unknown force, some puppeteer god, decided to pull my strings and leave James dangling. Maybe I prayed longer. Maybe my prayers were more worthy than his. Maybe I worked harder, smarter. Maybe I'm just a better person. Maybe. I wonder how many maybes James has added up. How many what ifs, should haves and if onlys? Find the total and you measure the distance between us.

I could tell you about prison, what the hopelessness and regret does to a boy's face. I could tell you about how grog and dope makes him happy. I could tell you about too many beatings, taken and given. I could tell you about me: expensive meals and flash hotels, nice houses and fine cars. I could tell you a lot of things that would make you pity him and praise me, or even like him and dislike me. There are a lot of tales about our lives, as I'm sure the goldfish — if he could talk — would tell you. He could tell you about every contour of his bowl, every rock and fern, every meal and every fish that swam and died alongside him, or he could tell you about the bowl, the only fact that matters to his existence. To James — to me — our goldfish bowl is our blackness: where we find refuge, how successfully we pass our days matter less than the fact we'll never live outside the bowl.

There was a time when the ledger tipped in his favour. At school James was a star. He was better looking than me, a better footballer than me, tougher, stronger, more daring and smarter. James was a leader; we looked up to him. I was lucky to be his friend. Our families went way back. My grandparents lived for a time with his mum and dad, when both of our families were trying to make it off the mission. James was the new baby for a new life. He was a late baby for Johnny and Hazel, and late babies are hope's gift. James knew how black lives could end; he knew that ambition and talent too often equalled disappointment. His brother — or at least his brother's memory — was all the reminder James needed. James's brother was the first Aborigine to finish high school in Griffith; he went from the playground to the mission, started drinking heavily and in just a few years was dead. Now as I take that second look at James across the church I think that my old friend could count at least one success: he's better at dying than his brother, he's made it last longer.

I don't know what these people think of me. So many of them say they're proud of me, and that just makes it worse. They should be suspicious, they should see me as a fraud; at least then I could justify myself. But they don't. They smile and open their arms and quietly condemn me to my guilt. Only yesterday I sat with my cousin Lex as he celebrated his forty-third birthday. Actually it wasn't a celebration, just an excuse for a drink. Forty-three years of memories, like seeing his mother's body dragged from an irrigation channel or saying goodbye to his father in hospital as he shat out what remained of his liver. He cried then he laughed about our life as kids, about spotlighting rabbits and sitting in his room while he proudly laid out his cadet's uniform. Now he's an old man, and I'm still young. He'll die before me — maybe before my forty-third birthday — and his death will mock my success.

I am a white success. In my whiteness I've gained the world, yet lost something of myself. I can't pretend to be a black success, there's really no such thing. I measure my life by your education, your jobs, your money, your houses, your cars. I'm an example of all that success can bring; in me white Australia buys back its guilty conscience. Now I can call myself a role model, join the ranks of those other comfortable blacks who tell themselves their lives make a difference. Sometimes I wonder if we don't offer a way up . . . just a way out. Somewhere in this church there's another me: the me who didn't leave Griffith, who looks like a 37-year-old blackfella should look. Somewhere James and I have traded places, I have to believe that. Not because of the promise of a better fate for James, but because I need to reassure myself I've just been lucky, that I haven't deliberately deserted him.

I feel like the immigrant's son, returning to his father's country. I see myself in these faces, but they're reflections of where I've been, where I'm from, but not where I'm going. These lives are measured in inches, I total mine in miles. I don't belong here any more, so I return only for funerals. Eventually — and it won't be long — all will be dead and I won't come here again. I'll sing for the last time that other hymn we sing at funerals: 'In the sweet by and by we will meet on that beautiful shore.'

Fifty years, that's all Laurie Johnson had. Fifty years to learn the immutable sum of our existence: black = death. If we stay black we don't live long; it's simple. But Laurie isn't a statistic, he's a life, like so many other black lives lived hard and short and then given a Christian burial. Laurie was a patriot and he died a patriot's death; in a better world I'd write a myth rather than a eulogy. Laurie's the fulfilment of prophesy: Australia's doomsday prediction of our extinction. Yes, he deserves a Christian burial.

We gained our faith from fear, not love. We worshipped not the defiant Christ who trashed the temple but the beaten figure on the cross who cried, 'My God, my God, why have you forsaken me?' Why wouldn't we, too, feel forsaken? Ours was the faith slandered by that philosophical anti-Christ Friedrich Nietzsche as one of 'subjection, self-derision, and self-mutilation'. Ours was a teasing God who promised eternity for our earthly suffering and called it a fair trade. This was a faith of straighteners, thin men who'd spent too much time in the shade of the prison house, the factory or the cotton field.

The Methodists made their conversions in blind alleys and amongst losers. The smokestacks of industrial Britain were the ideal cover for a religion that could welcome both master and slave and still not rupture society's foundations. The command to render unto Caesar what is Caesar's comforted the bourgeoisie while the proletariat trusted God would indeed take care of what was left. Subordination was gilded with the morality of the work ethic. In the words of historian E.P. Thompson, 'Not only the sack, but also the flames of hell might be the consequence of ill-discipline at work. God must be the most vigilant overlooker of all.'

As Methodism subverted the workers to the new machinery, so it distorted the personalities of its followers and discouraged ambition by weakening the poor from within. Joy was associated with sin and guilt, and pain with the image of a suffering Christ on the cross, the measure of goodness. Repentance and active submission to God formed the only path to his grace. Thompson described Methodism as a 'ritualised form of psychic masturbation', and portrayed its followers as a collection of 'religious invalids'.

> Within the Church itself there was a constant emotional drama of backsliders, confessions, forays against Satan, lost sheep; one suspects that the pious sisterhood, in particular, found in this one of the great 'consolations' of religion.

This religion of the defeated found willing converts, too, in the plantation fields of the American south. African slaves enduring a complete loss of liberty and toiling in the fields for little reward saw in the religion's teachings some hope of redemption in the afterlife. As Eugene Genovese tells us in *Roll, Jordan, Roll*, his epic history of slavery, the blacks found hope of deliverance in biblical heroes like Moses, Jonah and Daniel.

The slaves adjusted Methodism to their way of life. After a day in the fields the slave huts at night became the birthplace of a new Afro-Christian syncretism. This was seen most clearly in their ingenuity in incorporating cultural expressions that would otherwise appear antithetical to strict Methodism. The most obvious example was the shouting and dancing that characterised their religious celebration. According to Genovese the slaves, once converted, stopped their sinful dancing and went instead to the praise house. What the blacks did within the walls of their church may have looked like dancing, but because they had become Christians it couldn't be; it was 'shouting'.

> . . . the blacks convinced themselves that they did not dance the shout, for as everyone knows you cross your feet when you dance; and since they did not tolerate crossing of feet, they clearly were not dancing.

Uncle Tom could doff his cap at the Massa and laugh to himself that even his tormentor would one day face judgment. But if religion made suffering tolerable, it came at the cost of revolt. This was a faith of the status quo. The African slaves developed a spiritual base and even a new identity, but it also made them Americans. As James Baldwin would write hundreds of years later, 'the Negro has been formed by this nation, for better or for worse, and does not belong to any other'. When the black civil rights movement reached its zenith, they would fight as Americans and Christians, not Africans.

Thus the ingredients were right for the growth of Methodism among the remnants of the Aboriginal tribes that were being transformed by the new Australian nation. Charles Rowley contemplated the early efforts of Christians to civilise the Aborigines, noting their assumptions of Aboriginal subordination:

> For Christians at that time, 'welfare' for non-Christians meant conversion: it did not mean the right of free men to decide what they wanted to do, and then to find the opportunities to do it.

The early Wesleyan missions at Wellington Valley and Lake Macquarie had been established and abandoned by the time Charles Darwin published *On the Origin of Species* in 1859. The theory of evolution allowed settlers to see Aborigines as a prehistoric human relic, destined to die out. Missionaries, anthropologists and, in turn, policy makers saw their role as protecting the blacks from extinction. This attitude prevailed until the early twentieth century. The monthly reports of the Aboriginal Inland Mission depicted a battle with the forces of evil, as they struggled to lead the blacks out of darkness. The July 1909 issue of *Our A.I.M.* carried a verse on the front cover entitled 'Stir into Flame':

> *Stir me, O! stir me, Lord — I care not how,*
> *But stir my heart in passion for the world!*
> *Stir me to give, to go, but most to pray;*
> *Stir, till the blood-red banner be unfurled*
> *O'er lands that still in heathen darkness lie;*
> *O'er deserts where no cross is lifted nigh.*

And stir them the Lord did. The missionaries reported monthly success in converting Aborigines. A typical report from Bulgandramine mission in May 1919 read:

> Nine girls ranging in ages from eight to seventeen years have definitely accepted Jesus as their Saviour, and three young men also have come out on the Lord's side, for which we are most thankful.

By the 1930s the Aboriginal Inland Mission was reporting similar monthly conversion rates; at Condobolin in April 1932 seventeen adults and three children gave their hearts to the Lord. The strongest effort was aimed at the young, with the missionaries campaigning for the Aborigines Protection Board to be given greater powers to intervene for the children's welfare. In July 1909 *Our A.I.M.* argued that the board:

> . . . may be vested with power to rescue these children from what is nothing but evil, idleness and disaster and to give them a chance to be useful and honest members of the community.

To that end the missionaries had already established a children's home at Singleton in New South Wales to 'rescue the young half-caste girls from their evil surroundings'.

The new generation of Aboriginal Christians, like their counterparts among the working poor of England and the black slaves of the American south, saw their faith couched in terms of a repressive morality. Their religion was based around a strict code that eschewed vices such as gambling and drinking. Converts lived with the ever present fear of backsliding. An Aboriginal man, Jack Campbell, testified to his faith at the Terry-Hie-Hie mission in northwest New South Wales in June 1919. The missionaries reported:

> He gave a plain, straight and helpful message to the people. He told them how the Lord had delivered him from the power of sin and he reminded them of how he had gambled and used loaded dice, and spun two-headed pennies, and also how he had

> been addicted to the evil drink; but now the Lord had taken away the desire for those things.

Gambling was seen as one of the great scourges of the missions, even greater than the demon drink. In July 1909 *Our A.I.M.* reported that gambling is the gospel's greatest foe: 'Numbers are bound by Satan hand and foot, heart and head, in the bounds of this fascinating, venomous, demoralising vice, who never touch the drink.'

The missionaries cast themselves as redeemers battling the evil forces of the devil. Their reports often strayed into melodrama, missionaries seeking out evildoers, praying for their souls and keeping a watchful eye an any 'strange Aboriginals lurking about'.

> In a day or two the rattle of the coins proves too much, and the weak ones are enticed, and the conflict is renewed. It is sharper than ever this time, but ultimately the Lord again conquers. And so it goes on. Sometimes the victory is final and complete and gambling is forever stamped out in that camp. Again, like an ugly monster it rears its head repeatedly, so that there is one long strain, and if for a time there is a slackening of watchfulness, the dreaded hiss is heard again.

E.P. Thompson wrote that the great Methodist recruitment of the 1790s–1830s was forged out of despair. He asks: how was it that British Methodism could have such success as the religion of both the exploiter and the exploited? The same question could be posed in Australia. The answer lies in the blacks' inherent acceptance of their subordination. By the early 1900s the traditional symbols of authority had been usurped, the settlers and missionaries had then set the boundaries in which Aboriginal lives would be played out, and approval and recognition were accorded to those who best assimilated the new value system. While the missions were oppressive, restricted environments, they were also havens from a hostile, unwelcoming white society, and the missionaries were sometimes benevolent figures. You can catch a glimpse of the caring attitude towards those who best conformed, in the sad story of 'a dear little dark boy' from Bulgandramine mission who died in Peak Hill hospital in October 1921. The missionaries grieved for the nine-year-old boy, whom they described as 'remarkably intelligent with perfect manners'. A missionary, Miss Taylor, recalled how she sat with him as he died:

> How he pleaded with me to take him and be his mother! It was very touching. He passed away on Wednesday morning and we laid him to rest Thursday afternoon. The little coffin was covered with flowers, there being a wreath from the matron and nurses.

These were the hard years of the 1930s and 1940s; here the black world as I knew it was taking shape.

This wasn't society nurtured on the Dreamtime, but one desperately seeking its whiteness. These weren't the lost tribes of historical imagination, they weren't suspended between their traditional culture and the forbidden world of the whites; they'd scavenged a society out of the scraps of both. For my people, the Wiradjuri, the ancient deity, Baiame, was interchangeable with the white Christ.

Even the not-so-devout blacks could no longer avoid Christianity's influence. The straitlaced Methodists had been joined by competing denominations, including the Pentecostalists who'd saved the souls of the Pacific Islanders. Dr Malcolm Calley confirmed the extent to which Aborigines in New South Wales had embraced Christianity in his study of race relations on the north coast. He found that blacks practised an evangelical form of Christianity as a 'reaction against the inferior status assigned to them by the whites'. He found that the Aboriginal Pentecostalism resembled Melanesian cults in identifying traditional deities within Christianity. He also discovered that in religion Aborigines found an authority and a control over their lives lacking elsewhere:

> Religion provides the only avenue of leadership among the Bandjalung. Within the Pentecostal sect an Aborigine can achieve status and authority and make decisions without reference to white outsiders.

My pa, Cecil Grant, was raised amongst the missions that sprang up in what had been Wiradjuri country. He grew up hearing the stories of his father's life on the massive properties of Merriganowry and Grantwood outside Cowra. The injustice of the black Grants' dispossession of their land, while their white cousins prospered, burned deep in young Cecil's soul. Years later, during the Depression, he and his brother Seth walked onto the Grant property looking for work. Failing to notice the family resemblance in the black faces of his cousins, the property owner introduced them to the woodheap, paid them for their work and sent them on their way, none the wiser.

Cecil Grant looked at the work of the missionaries and saw the promise of justice and equality in a religion that offered salvation and grace regardless of colour. By the time he was married to my grandmother, Josie Johnson, he was living on Condobolin mission and had become what the church quaintly called a 'native worker'. In April 1932 he gave the sermon at a mission service. *Our A.I.M.* described it as a 'beautiful message based on Isaiah 1, 18'. A reading of this and subsequent verses reveals much about the attitudes which had shaped Aboriginal society and its political expression.

> *'Come now let us reason together,'*
> *says the Lord.*
> *'Though your sins are like scarlet,*
> *they shall be white as snow;*

> *though they are red as crimson,*
> *they shall be like wool.*
> *If you're willing and obedient,*
> *you will eat the best from the land;*
> *But if you resist and rebel,*
> *you will be devoured by the sword.'*

The choice of this passage reveals a man who realises his people's future lies within Australian society. My grandfather had faith that the Lord would deliver them, as Moses had delivered the Israelites to the promised land. It is the same hopeful fatalism that flourished among the African slaves in America. Only obedience to God and, implicitly, the law would secure justice; resistance and rebellion were to be avoided for fear of further destruction.

My grandfather earned his equality in the trenches of Tobruk during World War II. He certainly practised what he preached. Life as a blackfella on a mission controlled by managers and the Welfare Board would never again be an option. He moved his family away from Condobolin and onto the fringes of the rich fruit-growing town of Griffith. His children attended the local white school, and he became the first Aborigine to find work on the local shire council. Cecil Grant aspired to the best that white society could offer him; he was, by the broadest definition, assimilated.

Assimilation is an ugly word amongst Aborigines today; it's a word to be whispered or better still exchanged for some less loaded synonym. It's a byword for treachery, yet I can't look upon my grandfather with shame. A house uptown, white neighbours, white workmates — this was his way out, yet this is not the brave story of Aboriginal resistance so many fashion for themselves today. Some would prefer to see him as a victim — that's too convenient and a greater insult to his memory than to accuse him of being a traitor.

My grandfather was not alone. In New South Wales a new Aboriginal political voice was being heard, one that eschewed its tribal past. Progressive Associations were formed and reached out to the whites. In the words of two of the movement's leaders, William Ferguson and Jack Patten, 'We have no desire to go back to primitive conditions of the Stone Age. We ask you to teach our people to live in the Modern Age, as modern citizens.' Aborigines did not wish to be regarded with 'sentimental sympathy like koala bears', they said.

The leader of the Victorian-based Australian Aborigines League, William Cooper, campaigned along similar lines. Cooper argued that blacks were sufficiently 'civilised' to warrant their 'uplift to the full culture of the British race'. Like Patten and Ferguson, Cooper was contributing a black point of view to the debate that had raged since colonisation and accelerated during the later part of the nineteenth century: were Aborigines civilised or an ancient form of humanity destined for extinction?

The three most prominent Aboriginal leaders of the 1930s, Ferguson, Patten and Cooper, were all products of the mission system. In the case of Ferguson and Cooper, much of their claim for justice and equality was based on what they saw as their God-given right. Cooper argued for Aborigines to be given land not only to improve their economic position, but also as recognition of their 'divine right'. Cooper, along with my great-great-grandfather, Frank Foster, had been among the first Aboriginal children rounded up and taken to Reverend Daniel Mathews's Maloga mission. Frank's sister Bella would marry into the Atkinson family of which Cooper was a member. Cooper learnt his lessons well, not only converting to Christianity, but recognising that his future was best assured as a fully functioning member of the economic mainstream of Australia. The missionaries had instilled in Cooper an ambivalence towards his Aboriginal culture. He wrote that the lifestyle of his tribal forebears had been corrupted, and that the white man offered a 'wonderful new world' that blacks must be allowed to join.

As with my great-great-grandfather Frank, William Cooper aspired to white prosperity: Frank wished to be a teacher; William saw himself as a farmer. In 1887 Cooper and his brother, John Atkinson, wrote letters to the Aborigines Protection Board requesting grants of land to farm wheat. They were part of a state-wide push by blacks for land which would enable them to join the burgeoning rural capitalist economy. My great-grandfather Bill Grant successfully petitioned the Aborigines Protection Board for land outside Cowra in 1892, hoping to emulate his white cousins who were the wealthiest land-holders in the district. He was part of a push by Aborigines of his generation to claim vacant land. For a time they succeeded. Historian Heather Goodall estimates that of thirty-one reserves created by the New South Wales government between the 1860s and 1884, twenty-five came about as a result of Aboriginal agitation. This strategy of Aborigines demanding land continued up to the formation of the Aborigines Protection Board in 1887.

The Aboriginal farmers appeared to be the fulfilment of the white man's dream of civilising the blacks. Governor Macquarie had attempted to establish Aboriginal fishing villages around Sydney, and by the 1840s the British Secretary of State for Colonies, Earl Henry Grey, saw special Aboriginal reserves as great training grounds for the blacks' ultimate absorption into society. As Goodall says:

> Grey saw these small reserves as being the tools for forcing major social and cultural change, to transform Aboriginal landowners into the mythologised agrarian ideal of yeoman farmers.

Almost a hundred years later, Aborigines still saw their future as emulating the white landowners. The late 1930s Aboriginal newsletter *Abo Call*, edited by

Jack Patten, carried the slogan: '"Farms for Aborigines" is our cry'. Yet the blacks of Patten's era had been cheated out of their inheritance by a second wave of Aboriginal dispossession. Like the Native Americans and their treaty lands, Aborigines in New South Wales believed the reserve land was theirs forever, a gift from the Crown. As with the Native Americans, Aborigines only held their land as long as the whites didn't want it. The loss of their lands a second time was a cruel blow; hadn't they become farmers as the white man wished? Didn't they have a divine right to their land, to their economic security?

If William Cooper grew up in an era when Aborigines were gaining some measure of economic independence, Bill Ferguson came of age in a far more repressive period. Ferguson was born to a Wiradjuri woman, Emily Ford, and her Scottish husband, William Ferguson senior. After his mother died, young Bill was moved with his brothers and sisters to the mission at Warrangesda, the place established by the ill-fated missionary John Gribble. There he grew up alongside many of my own family, including my great-grandmother, Florence 'Nanny Cot' Foster.

Between 1895 and 1910 Bill Ferguson saw Aboriginal aspirations for autonomy come under siege from a constellation of forces, including racism, a white land grab, the increasing control of the Aborigines Protection Board, and the implementation of the *Aborigines Protection Act* of 1909 with its emphasis on dispersal and the removal of children.

Aborigines living on reserves created during the 1860s to 1890s had enjoyed a degree of freedom and control over their lives; they were soon to be reminded of the extent of their dispossession and powerlessness.

In the 1890s a severe depression, followed by a drought, placed stress on already fragile Australian race relations. Aborigines who had been working in the rural economy found themselves unemployed and with no access to the dole. For many the only choice was starve or retreat to the reserves under the control of the Protection Board, where at least they would receive basic rations. At the same time white prejudice was hardening. Many townsfolk wanted Aborigines out of sight and out of mind. They lobbied the board to use the reserves to enforce segregation. White parents banded together to shut Aboriginal students out of local public schools, claiming, amongst other things, that their children were at risk of disease carried by their black classmates. Aboriginal parents began petitioning for their own reserve-based schools; by 1909 there were twenty-seven black-only schools across the state.

With more and more Aborigines being forced onto reserves, more pressure was placed on reserve farmers, reducing their self-sufficiency. The board also felt the financial strain, exacerbated by having to employ managers and schoolteachers. The increase in government authority was something new to many Aborigines who'd lived free of state control. Blacks found themselves under the gaze of a New South Wales government keenly eyeing the repressive policies already in place in Victoria. The Victorian *Aborigines Act* 1886 was aimed at dividing the black community, separating families and driving so-called half-castes off the reserves. In New South Wales, the emphasis of the *Aborigines Protection Act* of 1909 was not on protecting Aboriginal lands but on separating children from their families so they would ultimately become like whites.

The end of the depression and the drought saw whites demanding more and more land, enviously eyeing the Aboriginal reserves. For a time the Protection Board defended the blacks, but by 1911 the board was actively leasing land to whites to boost its dwindling coffers. Aborigines who had previously worked their own land, as at Cummeragunja, had their property resumed by the board and were reduced to employees, toiling for the board's profit. The end of World War I also saw an increased demand for land as soldiers returned home to be resettled. The hopes of a generation of Aborigines for justice and economic independence, for the chance to take their place alongside whites, were dashed — not because the blacks didn't want to embrace assimilation, but because whites wouldn't let them. The loss of Aboriginal reserve lands accelerated. According to Heather Goodall, between 1916 and 1927:

> The area of reserve lands was slashed from 10 500 hectares to 5200 hectares . . . Most were lost

altogether or leased out to whites, making them just as inaccessible to the Aboriginal farmers.

In 1938, William Cooper, Bill Ferguson and Jack Patten masterminded an Aboriginal Day of Mourning to coincide with the commemoration of 150 years of white settlement in Australia. It was a brilliant publicity stroke, and the photograph of Ferguson and Patten surrounded by Aboriginal children carrying signs demanding citizenship is seared into the memory of Aborigines today. This was not simply a protest over the loss of Aboriginal lands and liberty, but a plea, yet again, for Australians to accept Aborigines as equals.

Ferguson was a devout Christian and had also been an active unionist. He courted support among left-wing Christian groups as well as seeking help, with Patten, from the Communist Party of Australia. Many historians have viewed Ferguson as someone who was more interested in equality than a recognition of Aboriginal culture, yet by 1938 he was becoming a proponent of black unity. Ferguson angered some white supporters, who accused him of separatism, by banning white membership of the Aborigines Progressive Association and making the Day of Mourning open to Aborigines only. Aboriginal patience was showing signs of wearing remarkably thin.

William Cooper, too, exhausted all political avenues to win support for Aboriginal justice and in 1935 formed the Aborigines Advancement League. The League had nine major demands, including the granting of full citizenship to civilised Aborigines and the setting aside of parliamentary seats for Aboriginal people. Cooper had been influenced by the experience in New Zealand, where Maoris had been granted four parliamentary seats in 1867. Cooper, like Ferguson, saw Aboriginal advancement not in terms of race, but civilisation. He organised a delegation to visit the prime minister, Robert Menzies, and then sought to petition King George V to draw attention to his people's plight. Cooper worked on the petition for several years, and between 1933 and 1935 gathered the signatures of over 1800 Aborigines from across the country. Cooper told a journalist, 'If we cannot get full justice in Australia we must ask the king. Some tell us the king has no power in these things, but we shall try anyway.'

But the king never saw the petition; the federal Cabinet examined it and decided to 'take no further action'.

Aboriginal anger spilled over in the most spectacular fashion with a black walk-off from the Cummeragunja mission in 1939. The people at Cummeragunja had at one time enjoyed control over their land, working successfully as farmers, but now tension was at boiling point. The Aborigines had grown fearful of an outbreak of polio after one boy was struck down with the disease, housing was poor and there was a chronic shortage of water. Such conditions were common on board-controlled reserves across New South Wales. The Great Depression of the 1930s, like the depression of the 1890s, had forced more blacks onto the reserves in search of rations. Under the restrictive laws of the time, the reserves became places of great suffering. William Cooper repeatedly wrote to the New South Wales premier complaining about the conditions at Cummeragunja, even inviting him to inspect the reserve for himself. His people grew frustrated as Cooper failed to arouse any support.

The situation at Cummeragunja was made worse by a manager, A.J. McQuiggan, whom the blacks described as arrogant and uncaring. McQuiggan carried a rifle and openly made threats of violence. The Aborigines raised a petition calling for the manager's sacking, but the board sent it back to McQuiggan himself, who defiantly posted it on the door of the reserve office. Jack Patten arrived at the mission to help orchestrate the political struggle, along with his brother George. On Friday, 3 February 1939, the blacks finally decided to walk off the mission.

Two hundred Aborigines crossed the river into Barmah in Victoria, and held out for nine months. During that time Patten was accused in the media of being an agitator, even working for the Nazi Party. Senior board members finally convinced the dissidents to return, with the promise of an inquiry, but they were met only with intimidation and reprisals from McQuiggan. Again the people walked off, but this time the board convinced the Victorian government to withhold food and ban the children from attending the local school. Thus a group of Aborigines was forced to live in exile, deprived of their liberty and their home. McQuiggan was ultimately sacked, but it was too little too late.

My ancestors had been violently dispossessed, then exterminated, their families torn apart and scattered across the land to eke out a living however they could. The remnants were told to become civilised, to farm the land, educate their kids and convert to Christianity. Still we were denied our chance to find justice, to be treated equally. My family was locked up on reserves, endured the complete loss of their liberty and had their children taken from them. Despite all of that, in the 1930s we were still asking white society to let us in, to let us become citizens. But a new hardness was appearing that would shape the next generation of black political leaders; it's glimpsed in the words of William Cooper, a man who had believed in British justice, but would die disillusioned. In a letter to the premier he wrote, 'We are not an enemy people and we are not in Nazi concentration camps. Why should we then be treated as though we are?'

Australia's whiteness breaks our hearts. It teases us and mocks us, it tempts the likes of me, and it shuns the likes of James and Lex. My grandfather and Bill Ferguson and Jack Patten and William Cooper, our blessed peacemakers, believed they'd see God. Now, too many of their sons and daughters know only a hell that puts them in their graves before their time.

In a new century my family stands by the grave of yet another Aboriginal man to die tragically young, a man who would live his life struggling for a place to belong. And again we sang our hymn of hope.

I will cling to the old rugged cross,
and exchange it some day for a crown.

9

Fightin' from the Losin' End

A dog starv'd at his master's gate
Predicts the ruin of the state
WILLIAM BLAKE

He can laugh about it now, a quarter of a century later. This is a mischievous laugh, head bowed, imperceptible except for the gentle rocking of his shoulders below his mane of grey hair. In fact I'm wrong to call it a laugh, this is more of a sneer; if you gave it a name you'd spell it in capital letters: F–U–C–K Y–O–U!

Bob McLeod sits like an emperor on the verandah of his house outside Nowra on the New South Wales south coast. To meet Bob is to wrestle with the man and his legend. Most mortals, no matter their degree of fame, can't sustain a legend; the legend wins out, dwarfing the individual whose deeds first fed the myth. But Bob is not so easily reduced. He at least fights his legend to a respectable loss on points.

'Age shall not weary them, nor the years condemn.' The ode could have been written for Bob McLeod. The brave boys of Gallipoli left their youth intact on the battlefield where they fell; Bob buried his within his soul, there forever to remain an angry young man.

He's named his property Bellefield Estate. The image the name conjures up sits perfectly with this place of serenity, shrouded by gently rolling hills and reached by a winding dirt road. For Bob, it's a serenity hard won, but if the years have softened his rage, if his shoulders are a little rounded and his midriff filling out, they can't hide the fire inside. To be around Bob is to be uneasy; like walking on broken glass. You know you'll get cut, the only question is how deeply. I had arranged to meet Bob in town earlier in the day at a Christmas party for local Aboriginal children. Bob invited me back to his house for dinner and innocently I offered him a lift: mistake number one. Don't assume anything with Bob McLeod.

'Whaddaya think — I'm a broke blackfella; haven't got a car?' he replied, just enough irritation in his voice to unsettle me.

For a moment I was struck with the fear of a child taken home to his parents by the police; the anticipation is far worse than any punishment. Slowly his lips curled into a smile; he let me off the hook. The years, though, have left Bob with an inscrutable demeanour, and I'm still not convinced he was joking.

Now we are reliving another moment, far more spectacular, when he struck fear into the heart of a nation: that instant when the future of race relations in this country rested with a man feasting on his own rage, his mind distorted by drugs and alcohol, unable to measure his thoughts, control his actions — a man with a gun in his hands.

'It's funny when ya think about it,' Bob says now, with no hint of irony.

Funny? It was 1974 and Bob McLeod had hatched a plan to arrest the head of the Department of Aboriginal Affairs, Barrie Dexter.

'I walked into the department and asked for Dexter; his secretary asked if I had an appointment. "Yeah," I said.' With that Bob cocks his fingers in the shape of a gun, imitating how he placed a real, loaded .38 to the head of the terrified receptionist that day.

McLeod marched through the office, finally confronting a senior departmental officer.

'I told him I was arresting him for the murder of black children. He was shittin' himself; I thought he going to have a heart attack and all I could think was don't die now, ya bastard, I want the pleasure of killin' ya meself.'

Even now Bob's enjoying this, he has the kind of glee in his eye that fat middle-aged men get reliving their youthful sporting glories. The difference is they tend to exaggerate; Bob has no need. The swagger of an outlaw suits him.

'I was at the tent embassy at Parliament House,

see, and I said to a group of 'em; "Come on, let's shake up these bastards." So anyway we jump in the car and we stopped at a pub for a drink, that's when I pulled the gun, you shoulda seen it, there was blackfellas goin' everywhere. In the end it was me an' Tar Boy went in there.'

As Bob tells it now, this was part of a war — a war he had declared on white Australia.

One hundred years ago another Aborigine embarked on his own campaign of terror; the tale of Jimmy Governor has historical parallels with Bob McLeod. On the cold winter night of 20 July 1900, Jimmy Governor and his uncle, Jack Underwood, bludgeoned five people, women and children, to death with tomahawks and nulla-nullas at a farmhouse at Breelong, near Dubbo. Governor had been working and living on the property, owned by the Mawbey family. It had been an uneasy coexistence, made more tenuous by Jimmy's marriage to a white woman, Ethel Page.

The Governor murders stand as a stark, tragic exemplar of the worst aspects of race relations at that time in Australia. It is a story that encompasses the dual Aboriginal responses to colonisation — resistance and accommodation — and highlights the eventual futility of both.

Jimmy and Ethel had suffered taunts about their interracial marriage and their mixed-breed child. There had also been a dispute over rations; Jimmy claimed Mrs Mawbey had overcharged him for their supplies. Ethel had been complaining to Jimmy about a lack of food and about the insults she'd suffered from the Mawbeys and their schoolteacher, Ellen Kerz. On the night of the attack, the mood in the Governors' camp was tense; Ethel and Jimmy had been arguing. Finally Jimmy set off with his uncle, his mind bent on justice. He first went to the shearing shed to confront Mr Mawbey, winning a promise of an increase in rations. Full of his victory, Governor and Underwood made for the Mawbey household to settle his differences with 'the missus'. As Governor later testified:

> So I said to my wife, I said, 'We'll go up and see Mrs Mawbey about those words she's been saying about us.' I says to my wife, 'I'll make her mind what she's talking about. I'll pull her to court if she doesn't watch herself.'

The confrontation quickly turned nasty, Jimmy Governor demanding an apology for the racial slurs. As Jimmy would testify at his trial, Mrs Mawbey and Miss Kerz sneered at him, sending him into a frenzy. He remembered hitting the women, but after that he said he recalled nothing. When the attack was over, bodies were strewn around the homestead, the floors and walls awash with blood. Others were killed as they tried to escape, their bodies left by the roadside. Jimmy, his brother Joe and their uncle, Jack

Underwood, then set out on a rampage of murder and robbery. It would end with Jimmy's capture three months later, after a manhunt covering three thousand kilometres and involving two thousand men. Joe Governor was killed in the pursuit, Jacky Underwood arrested and sentenced to hang, while Jimmy, too, would ultimately swing for his crimes. He remained unrepentant, saying only, 'I have made a name for myself.'

While the Breelong Massacre, as it became known, is captivating in itself, it becomes more fascinating as a window into a world that could have fostered such a crime. It's convenient to characterise the murders in purely racial terms, ascribing a cultural explanation for Jimmy's actions. Thomas Keneally's fictionalised version, *The Chant of Jimmie Blacksmith*, was a bestseller and eventually a film, portraying Jimmy as a metaphor for Aboriginal dislocation and powerlessness. Historian Henry Reynolds dismisses a racial motive, depicting the crime as the actions of a young man estranged from his culture, infatuated with the derring-do of bushrangers like Ned Kelly and frustrated by his poverty. Both interpretations fail to capture the complexities and contradictions that were recasting Aboriginal identity and lifestyles during the period.

Jimmy Governor lived at a time when his participation in Australian society, particularly the rural capitalist economy, was contingent on his repudiation of his Aboriginal heritage. To this he was happy to acquiesce, as many historians have revealed. Ethel testified that Jimmy did not like being called a blackfella and Jimmy boasted at his trial that, 'I was never a loafer, like some blackfellows. I always worked, and paid for what I got, and I reckon I'm as good as a white man.'

His determination to live like a white person hooked him on the horns of a fatal dilemma. The more he 'acted' white, the more whites rejected him; in their eyes he was, at best, mimicking them.

In his eagerness to remake himself in the image of his colonisers, Jimmy Governor appears as a human pinwheel of colours seeking to merge into one. He imagined a synthesis of the white and black sides of his nature, believing he could outgrow his blackness and emerge fully grown, like a child emerging into adolescence, as a 'civilised' being. He didn't count on the synthesis being so repugnant. His efforts were pathetic: not only was he doomed to be rejected by whites, he embodied an Aboriginal society that had become unhinged, a people who struggled to express themselves outside of the prism of white Australia.

'I am other than what I would wish to be, and I am determined by what I deny.' In the words of the great French writer Michel de Certeau, I find a road map to my own identity. I can see clearly the forces that make all of us who or what we are. Certeau goes backstage in the creation of history; he separates the generations by stating boldly, 'I can't be that.' For Jimmy

Governor, 'I can't be that' means being an Aborigine. He is determined by the denial of his very blackness.

Governor's story is a more spectacular representation of the bind all of his black countrymen found themselves in. From the moment the British flag was planted on Australian soil, we were encapsulated within colonisation. Our identity ceased to be a purely Aboriginal one, or more precisely an isolated tribal one, and became one of being British subjects. The overwhelming beliefs that we had no political or legal claim on our land and that as a people we were an archaic race formed the boundaries of our existence. Aboriginal identity, in any traditional sense, was untenable: Aboriginal customary law was not recognised, and there were no records of our births, deaths or marriages.

Adoption of a 'white' identity was the only currency for participating in Australian society. Christianity and agriculture completed this new civilisation. But there was no denying black skin, and that, together with a lifestyle unacceptable to white society, more often than not disqualified Aborigines. We were left with an invidious choice: resist, as many Aboriginal people did, or reach an accommodation. Jimmy Governor's identity was not one based on his traditional inheritance, his reference points were laid down by white society and his ultimate salvation, so he believed, was in conforming.

Aborigines like Bob McLeod made heroes of people like Governor; in the eyes of militant blacks, Jimmy was a patriot. Jimmy bequeathed his neurosis to his modern-day acolyte, Bob McLeod. As McLeod held hostage the staff at the Department of Aboriginal Affairs he was acting on the same impulses that drove Jimmy, his ideological great-grandfather. This was a man acting out a deranged fantasy of black retribution, little aware that what he was doing was inhabiting one of the roles colonialism had conveniently laid out for him. He was a legitimate part of the very society he was railing against, his identity and his political activism drawn from the well of modern Australia, not an ancient, timeless Aboriginal past.

Bob McLeod's people are from Wreck Bay, an Aboriginal reserve on the New South Wales south coast. Like all Aborigines in the area the McLeods had felt the full brunt of white settlement. Traditional Aboriginal culture had given way to a new society: impoverished, and trapped between a black society they were no longer a part of and a white world that rejected them.

The lives of the south coast blacks, like Aborigines throughout the state, were tightly controlled by the Aborigines Protection Board, which could remove families from their homes, deny them rations and clothing, even assume control of wages and government benefits such as the family endowment. In most cases the Aboriginal families couldn't have a drink in a pub, could be denied schooling, and if they went to the movies they watched the screen from a specially roped-off section of the cinema. The best many Aborigines could hope for was work as itinerant fruit-pickers; the money they earned often squandered on alcohol to escape their wretched surroundings. As historians R.G. Castle and J.S. Hagan wrote, 'In all aspects of life they were subject to white authority. They were socially segregated and dependent on welfare, on white charity and benevolence.'

Amongst this community the McLeods were considered shining lights. Bob was a keen student and outstanding sportsman; his mother, Belle, a devout Christian, which won her respect from local townsfolk. By all measures the McLeod family was prime fodder for the government policy of assimilation, the dream of merging black families into white suburbs in the hope of eventually removing any trace of Aboriginality. Thus, in his teens, Bob, his mum and dad and five brothers and sisters found themselves in the ludicrously named Green Valley on Sydney's western outskirts.

Green Valley was a New South Wales Housing Commission social experiment. At a cost of £20 million a new suburb was created in 1961; three years later there were more than six thousand houses. Clinton Walker, in a profile of Bob McLeod in his book *Buried Country*, described it as a 'human dumping ground in a clay desert, just waiting to erupt'. Bob McLeod is more succinct: it was 'the dregs of society'. 'There was nuthin' there,' he tells me. 'They were puttin' us with white families who had nuthin' to begin with.'

Within a few years young Bob was running the streets. A big, tough lad, he knew how to use his fists. Added to the already potent cocktail of resentment, adolescent bravado and physical strength was a growing abuse of alcohol; he admits he was already drinking methylated spirits as a teen. By the time he was eighteen he was hauled before the courts on a charge of assault and robbery. As a first-time offender, Bob expected a good behaviour bond; but the judge had ideas of making an example of him, and McLeod found himself sentenced to five years in Berrima jail.

'There was a Scottish bloke I met in there; he said, "You want a bit of advice? Don't listen to any bastard in here, if they knew what they were talking about they wouldn't be in here in the first place",' Bob says.

For Bob McLeod jail was a reawakening. He knew he was a rebel, now he discovered his cause: Aboriginal injustice. Onto his growing awareness of black politics he welded a new identity fashioned out of the image of his people as victims. Bob worked in the prison library and he started to read: Charles Rowley's *The Destruction of Aboriginal Society* told him about the white invasion; about the decimation of Aboriginal tribes by disease; it told him about the massacres; the rape of black women; and about successive government policies aimed, at best, at smoothing the pillow of the dying Aboriginal race.

He also pondered his mother's religion, Christianity. He looked for answers in the Bible; he read Job and asked how it was that the 'evil man is spared the day of calamity, that he is delivered from the day of wrath'. If the sun also rises on the just and the unjust, Bob McLeod would seek his own justice; his would be Old Testament retribution: an eye for an eye. In 1968 Bob was released, an angry man. The years in prison had lit a fire under what had already been an explosive mix of bitterness and resentment. Australia, too, had changed; just the year before, a referendum had been passed recognising Aborigines in the census (we were no longer to be classed with the flora and fauna) and providing for the federal government to make laws for the improvement of Aboriginal welfare, supposedly ending the tyranny and neglect of various state regimes. But Bob had no need of white society; he would reject it as it had rejected him.

Casting aside his prison uniform, Bob dressed in the new style: the hip fauvistic fashions of the burgeoning Afro-American rebellion. It was not just a mode of dress, but a political lingua franca which translated from the United States to the streets of Redfern in inner-city Sydney. Bob McLeod felt right at home amongst the new breed of militant young Aborigines. To them he wasn't a thug, an alco, a crim; he could fashion himself as a 'prisoner of war', his criminal record a badge of honour. He played football with the Redfern All Blacks, sang in pubs and continued to drink heavily. He fell in with kindred spirits among the nascent black leadership like Dennis Walker and Gary Foley. These were impatient men, no longer prepared, unlike their political progenitors, to wait for change; they modelled themselves on the American Black Panthers.

Black America had undergone a resurgence of racial pride during the 1960s. The lightning rod for much of it was one-time hustler and crim turned self-styled cleric in the Nation of Islam, the former Malcolm Little, who preferred to be known simply as Malcolm X. The X signified the theft of his African identity by the American slave masters. Malcolm X stood as a counter to the brotherly love and non-violent resistance preached by Dr Martin Luther King junior. Malcolm X spoke especially to the frustrated souls of the northern blacks; he spoke of the 'white devil' and advocated violence. For Malcolm X the liberation of the blacks could not be attained within colonialist America. Malcolm X could have been speaking for Bob McLeod. In late 1963 Malcolm X made a grassroots address to blacks, the sound waves of which resonated in Australia.

> And every time you look at yourself, be you black, brown, red or yellow, a so-called Negro, you represent a person who poses such a serious problem for America because you're not wanted . . . We have this in common: we have a common oppressor, a common exploiter and a common discriminator. But once we all realise that we have a common enemy then we reunite.

Malcolm X ridiculed those he branded 'Uncle Toms', those blacks who acquiesced to the whites. The Uncle Toms, he said, wanted de-segregation, they wanted to sit at the same lunch-counter, they wanted to love their enemy. Malcolm X asked if it was wrong to be violent defending black women and children; if it was right for America to draft blacks to fight in its wars, to use violence against others, then it was right for blacks to use violence in defence of their interests. The revolution Malcolm X favoured was a revolution based on land. Land, he said, was 'the basis of freedom, justice and equality'. The Gary Foleys, Dennis Walkers and Bob McLeods had found a revolutionary rhetoric for the age-old Aboriginal struggle for recognition of land rights.

By the time Malcolm X was gunned down at a rally in New York in 1965, his black apostles had spread far and wide. The Lowndes County Freedom Organisation had adopted the symbol of the black panther and become known colloquially as the Black Panther Party. The Student Non-violent Co-ordinating Committee had helped popularise the slogan 'Black Power'. In 1968 the Black American struggle was controversially highlighted to the world when athletes John Carlos and Tommy Smith stood astride the victory podium at the Mexico Olympics, their heads bowed and hands raised in a black-gloved, clenched-fist 'black power' salute in defiance of the American anthem. In Australia Aborigines formed their own version of the Panthers, and Gary Foley and

Dennis Walker were photographed mimicking the black-gloved salute.

Militant Aborigines in the late 1960s and early 1970s were radically distancing themselves from the William Coopers, Bill Fergusons and Jack Pattens of the 1930s, characterising the demands of the early activists for citizenship as appeasement of white hostility against blacks. Young Aborigines looked not to their grandfathers but to the radical blacks of America for inspiration.

Increasingly, Aborigines adopted many of the strategies of America's civil rights movement, most notably in Charles Perkins's Freedom Ride to end segregation in western New South Wales. This tumultuous period of activism also saw demand for recognition of urban Aborigines' claims to their traditional lands. Pastor Doug Nicholls, a long-time Aboriginal campaigner, asserted that 'Aborigines are not just another depressed social group, but an ethnic minority, descendants of the original land-holders with rights to land, to their culture and to a say in their destiny.'

Aborigines cast about for a unifying cause, a development of a pan-Aboriginal consciousness. One of those instrumental in the movement was another former prison inmate, Kevin Gilbert. Gilbert had been jailed for the murder of his white wife and had characterised the crime and his conviction as owing to Australian racism. Turning to writing, he quickly forged a literary reputation with his highly charged, polemical work. In his popular book *Because a White Man'll Never Do It*, he portrayed urban Aboriginal society as dislocated and estranged even from its own traditions:

> Underneath it all there is frustration, obsequious resentment, divided loyalties, uncertain values. There is no real belonging, no real identification except to misery. It is true that the modern Aborigine is sick, very sick.

Gilbert was identifying more than perhaps even he realised. He had isolated a lingering problem: how can you identify yourself when you don't know who or what you are? These were people who had suffered, who had been impoverished, and in some cases even imprisoned. Now they could rationalise their existence and oppression by excluding white society, which in turn Aborigines could claim had excluded them. To bolster their political campaign and strengthen their own identities, Aborigines needed to remind themselves and white Australia of their links to traditonal society. The opportunity arose in 1965 when the Gurindji people in the Northern Territory, led by Vincent Lingiari, walked off the British-owned Wave Hill cattle station, protesting against the working conditions and demanding wage justice.

The Gurindji action drew together the various elements of the burgeoning social activism in 1960s

Australia, attracting trade unionists, hippies interested in cultural diversity and non-conformity, and communists like the author Frank Hardy who wrote extensively about the Gurindji. As Heather Goodall surmised in *Invasion to Embassy*, the Gurindji would be all things to all people:

> The Gurindji could be characterised not only as industrial militants and traditional land rights campaigners but also as Australian nationalists battling against the British aristocracy and capitalist establishment.

To the Aborigines in the cities and towns of the south, the Gurindjis gave expression to their growing sense of a need for political unity. Malcolm X had reminded blacks in America that they had a common enemy; Kevin Gilbert did the same here. He drew links between the Gurindji struggle and the plight of detribalised, dispossessed urban blacks. All, he said, shared 'the fact of persecution by whites'.

In 1971 another Northern Territory land rights claim mobilised the militant Aboriginal movement. The Yirrkala people had challenged the setting up of a bauxite mine at the Gove Peninsula. The ensuing court action resulted in Mr Justice Blackburn delivering a judgment that struck at the very heart of the growing land rights push. He ruled that within Australian law there was no capacity to recognise Aboriginal property rights. The doctrine of *terra nullius* was upheld; Aborigines saw this as yet another dispossession.

By the early 1970s Aboriginal activists, modelling themselves on their black American counterparts, had established grassroots legal and medical services. Black delegations travelled to China, seeking international recognition for their plight and recognising in the communists a potential revolutionary lever. One activist, Sol Bellear, visited the Black Panthers in America; when he overstayed his visa, his 'brothers' smuggled him from house to house as he lived on the run from American authorities seeking to deport him.

At home, blacks surfed a wave of support on the back of anti-Vietnam protests and the anger over the South African Springboks rugby tour. Emerging from this period of intense activism was the plan to set up an Aboriginal tent embassy on the lawns of Parliament House in Canberra, an ingenious masterstroke that would graphically highlight the Aboriginal struggle and catapult black issues onto the front pages of the country's newspapers and onto television screens in every home in the nation. In the words of Aboriginal activist and journalist John Newfong, 'the mission has come to town'.

Bob McLeod was my window onto this world of political turmoil that would change my life in ways I could not possibly have imagined. Like thousands of Aboriginal families throughout the country, my family preferred to live quietly — making the most of what they had, and making no waves. Who needed attention, when the government could take away your children. These 'black radicals', as my parents called them, were just troublemakers. But Bob we couldn't ignore. Dad's sister Lorna was married to Bob McLeod's uncle, Bob Brown; that made us family — 'cousins'. I can remember hiding behind the door and peering around the corner when Bob was in the house; a big, hulking presence, a man who wore his already fearsome reputation like a loose coat. He cultivated a sense of black pride and liked to call my mum and dad 'brother' and 'sister'.

Bob naturally gravitated to the tent embassy. His uncle, Chicka Dixon, had been instrumental in masterminding the protest. Chicka, like Bob, was a former jailbird, and an alcoholic who had learnt his politics as a wharfie and member of the Waterside Workers' Federation. Chicka remembers attending his first black political meeting when he was in his teens, his motivation then was less about justice and more about meeting young black girls. For years, he says, he wandered in a drunken haze, in and out of prison; he admits he was heading for an early grave. The turning point came when Chicka was living in the long grass around the La Perouse reserve in Sydney; he was drinking heavily and, as he says, 'living and sleeping in my own shit'.

'One day I went up to me sister's place up 'ere on the mission, and she told me to have a bath and clean meself up,' he says. 'Anyway, I tried to have a shave and I was shaking so much — from the piss, ya know, the DT's they call it — I couldn't hold the razor to have a shave. Cut me face to pieces.'

As Kevin Gilbert said, the modern Aborigine was 'sick, very sick'. To Chicka, like Bob McLeod, the white man — the gubbah — was to blame. He quit the grog and became a political activist; 'That's what saved me,' he says. Soon Chicka was holding discussion nights with other militant blacks at his home. There they hatched the plan for the embassy. Gary Foley recalls they dubbed it the 'embassy' because 'Aborigines were aliens in their own land'. At first, Chicka says, they planned to occupy Fort Denison in Sydney Harbour as a symbolic act of colonisation, but that was jettisoned in favour of Canberra. The tent embassy hosted visits from the international media, Soviet diplomats, Canadian Indians, Native Americans and members of the Irish Republican Army. The activists had learnt the lessons of Malcolm X well, young Aborigine Michael Anderson warning, 'As soon as they start tearing up Arnhem Land we're going to start tearing up bits of Australia . . . our spiritual beliefs are connected with the land.'

The creation of the modern Aboriginal identity appeared complete. The sense of belonging Gilbert had said was lacking was fleshed out with allusions to tradition and so-called radical politics. Aborigines from the Northern Territory, the real blackfellas, were bused in to give the protest a sense of black unity. For Bob McLeod this was a place to feel at home; the growing threat of violence suited him as well. One placard read, 'Land Rights or Bloodshed'. Among the yards of film shot by television crews is a grainy black and white image of a young Bob, an imposing figure emerging from the smoke of the camp fires around the tents to scream down the lens of a camera, 'Get fucked, people of Australia!'

By 1973 Bob was back in jail, this time at Cooma. It was during this stint that McLeod's father, Arthur, burned to death in a house fire. Bob attended his dad's funeral at Wreck Bay in chains.

'A group of blokes here, me brothers and cousins, they were ready to bust me out,' he says, 'they had guns and everything. "Just tell us," they said, but "No," I said, "it's all right."'

Back in his cell Bob had time to brood. He hated white people, he blamed them for what had happened to him and for the death of his father. It was then that he made his declaration of war; he also wrote his first song, 'Wayward Dreams':

Because we are a part of this vast and
peaceful place,
Freedom then is a common thing for the
whole Aborigine race.
Why the white man tries to change our
way of life, it seems,
Is because we will not fit into his wayward,
scheming dreams.

This elegy is more than a lament, it is a statement of defiance. It couches Bob's new sense of identity in a romantic ideal of a traditional Aboriginal past he had never really shared in; it also rejects a white society that his family had tried to embrace when they posed, smiling, for photographers outside their new home at Green Valley.

Now here he was, just a year later, acting out a deranged black fantasy of retribution. The same forces that conspired to send Jimmy Governor on a murderous rampage — a sense of alienation and resentment — had Bob with a gun thrust into the mouth of a senior public servant. Outside, the office block was ringed with heavily armed Commonwealth police, ready, waiting, for the order to open fire. McLeod by then wanted to see just one man, the department's most senior Aboriginal officer, Charles Perkins.

'They were planning to get rid of Charlie, they thought he was dangerous, so I thought I'd show 'em there was an even more dangerous blackfella,' Bob said.

Charles Perkins had been a thorn in the department's side for years. His was the most outspoken black voice in the country. Unlike the radicals, Perkins positioned himself within the system, but he was no less impatient. In Perkins's mind Aboriginality was a qualification in the department, thus he was better equipped to run black affairs than any of the older, much more experienced, but white, politicians and bureaucrats. Perkins wanted Barrie Dexter's job as head of the Department of Aboriginal Affairs and to that end he'd crossed swords with the Minister for Aboriginal Affairs, Labor senator Jim Cavanagh. Relations between the black bureaucrat and the minister had rapidly deteriorated after Perkins questioned why Aborigines should take advice from yet another white man. As Perkins's future lay in the balance, the media carried threats of violent Aboriginal unrest if he was sacked. Undaunted, Perkins travelled the country, continuing his almost daily attacks on the administration of Aboriginal affairs.

Bob McLeod, too, had been up north and to Western Australia. He had seen the deplorable conditions his people had to endure and had his head filled with tales of white brutality. Now, acting as a self-styled freedom fighter, he believed he must exact revenge. Only McLeod truly knows how close we came to a bloodbath on that day, 1 March 1974, but there's no doubt he went to the department with the deadliest intent. In the end Perkins settled McLeod and his offsider, whom they called 'Tar Boy', and he reasoned that the charges against McLeod would be less serious if it was shown the gun was unloaded. They did a deal: Perkins put three bullets in each sock and led McLeod and his accomplice out. He later buried the bullets in his garden. Bob McLeod was politically too hot to handle; his lawyer argued that his clumsy attempt at terrorism was a charade with no violent intent. For his trouble, McLeod was given a $40 fine and placed on a good-behaviour bond for twelve months, a judicial anticlimax that at least for a time cauterised Bob's activism.

History, Michel de Certeau writes, 'can be construed as the gesture of a new beginning'. Bob McLeod turned to writing his own history in his songs. He interpreted his history, his life, as being traumatised by the act of dispossession, by the white theft of his land. He identified himself as an Aborigine to achieve a sense of belonging, oblivious to the reality that he was constructing an identity from the fragments of Aboriginal society that had been completely encapsulated in modern Australia. The Aboriginal identity is just one manifestation of an Australian identity. For many detribalised blacks, this effort to construct a meaningful world for themselves had often destructive consequences. Aboriginal pastor Ossie Cruise told Kevin Gilbert in *Living Black* how getting drunk substituted for a lost tribal ritual: 'the big thing was to be able to drink; for me to arrive at manhood was to be able to take a strong drink . . . I wanted to become a man. It was like an initiation ceremony.'

Bob, too, drank. He's lost many of the past twenty-seven years to a drunken haze. He may have walked with danger, he may have been boastful of black pride, but he also walked a lonely, self-destructive path. In his song 'Friendship Road' he wrote:

To be caught in the middle of no-man's land,
Not knowing which way to turn.

After the Department of Aboriginal Affairs hold-up, the aspiring terrorist turned storyteller. He carved out a new underground fame as a singer–songwriter; he played in pubs, cut a record and even appeared on television. Bob sang country music in the style of renegade performer Kris Kristofferson, he penned protest songs and often performed an ironic version of the hit 'Born Free'. Music writer Clinton Walker calls Bob McLeod the single most undervalued talent in Australian popular music history, describing him as 'sensual, a voice and presence oozing danger and sexuality, Bobby McLeod could have been our first black superstar'.

But Bob's talent and intellect were squandered in an orgy of booze, violence and sex. At one stage he and his brothers had over thirty assault charges against them. Along the way he fathered nine children to five different women.

'The only one I didn't have a kid with was my first wife and I married her on April Fools' Day, 1972,' he laughs.

He was drinking so much that he would lapse into delusions, sometimes seeing Aboriginal 'clever men', lawmen out to get him. This lifestyle was the cornerstone of his identity; it may not have liberated him, but it gave him someone to blame.

Bob McLeod's life invites quick, harsh judgment, and you won't get much argument from him. This is a man who knows what he's done; he confronts you with an honesty that's unnerving, leaving no place for regrets or lingering apologies.

'I couldn't change anything,' he says. 'I had to go through all of that to get here, where I am now.' He pauses for a moment before adding with a chuckle, 'Why wipe your arse twice?'

Bob McLeod's struggle, like Jimmy Governor's, is part of the struggle for grace by people we identify as Aborigines. Bob has searched inside himself and explored Aboriginal culture to give his life meaning. During the 1970s he underwent a secret and sacred Aboriginal initiation ceremony; later he travelled to America and endured the Native American sun dance. For four days men gather for the gruelling ritual: each morning they spend hours in a sweat lodge with the temperature set at a scorching 140 degrees, then they dance without food or water until sundown. Day after day, after day, after day; slowly the hundreds who start fall away, and those who are left truly are men.

'On the first day the men were all dancing as fast as they could, singing loudly, but a bloke next to me said, "Just follow me, get into a groove, barely move your feet,"' Bob recalls.

But the sweating and dancing wasn't everything; the ceremony wasn't complete. McLeod had two hooks placed into his chest and attached to ropes; slowly he was winched off the ground, suspended in air until the hooks ripped through his skin. Today Bob has rocks embedded in his elbows and thighs; he says it's part of a birthing process, a process of initiation. He will nurture the rocks in his body for fourteen years before, as he says, 'they're old enough' to be sent back into the world. It sounds extreme, but for him it works. Bob McLeod has not had a drink for fifteen years, he has spent many years running a healing centre in his hometown of Nowra, and has co-ordinated an Aboriginal dance group which travels the world, in demand from Italy to Taiwan.

Bob now speaks in terms of humanity, not just Aborigines. Healing, he says, comes from a connection to the Mother Spirit of the land, regardless of whether you happen to be black or white. His life can be seen as illustrative of the bind we are all in, particularly Aboriginal people.

Perhaps there's a more simple answer, one that owes itself to the ego-shattering street logic forged in the prison cells and back alleys where Bob grew up. As he says, 'I was born with a halo and an arsehole . . . when the halo gets too big, my arsehole closes up — that's when I know I'm full of shit.'

10

Irish Aborigine

A wet winter, a dry spring, a bloody summer and no king.

IRISH PROVERB

Belfast is the sort of place a man can find out who he is, and who he isn't. So it was for me. I'd flown in, full of the spirit of Michael Collins and Eamon De Valera. The two star-crossed rebels had fired my nascent revolutionary feelings when I read of the audacious 1916 Easter uprising. From the vantage point of a precocious yet idiotically naive teenager, their actions promised the hope of liberation. Never mind that the disenfranchised Irish Catholics enjoyed the advantage of numbers; never mind that they were armed to the eyeballs; that they had the backing of capitalists and communists alike; never mind that despite all of that they still failed. I imagined in my romantic reading of vainglorious Irish history a template for our own liberation.

At university I sat with my cadre of young black faux-rebels and talked of how a band of guerillas, just one hundred strong, could terrorise Australia. We wouldn't do it of course, we imagined ourselves as the intelligentsia; those hard-core mission blacks would avenge our injustice. How ridiculous. Avenge what? The fact that white Australia had paid for my education? That the university I attended created places especially for us? But I tasted injustice vicariously and comforted myself with high-minded statements like, 'The price of tyranny is eternal vigilance.' Mine was a three musketeers' credo of suffering: 'All for one, and one for all.' I may cringe now, but I don't apologise for my idealism; it fired the spirit and seared the soul.

To Irish fervour we added the fire and brimstone of the black American revolutionary Malcolm X, the courage and dignity of Dr Martin Luther King junior and the stoicism of Nelson Mandela to complete our cocktail of revolutionary rhetoric. Remember what Brother Malcolm said, we reminded ourselves: 'What do you call a black man with a PhD? . . . A nigger!' Yeah, that's right, we convinced ourselves. Then, as if to show our confusion and contradiction knew no bounds, we would quote the advocate of passive resistance, Dr Martin Luther King junior: 'judged not by the colour of their skin, but the content of their character'.

We were rebellious cherry-pickers. We'd pluck from the trees of any madman or despot who suited our fashion. We'd see merit in the anti-imperialist ravings of Libya's Colonel Gaddafi, the anti-Zionist terrorism of the Palestinian Liberation Organisation; we quoted from the Communist Manifesto and Mao's *Little Red Book*, even from *Mein Kampf*. One of our number ventured that Hitler's lunatic prescription for racial purity was correct. This from a person whose face betrayed as much European heritage as it did Aboriginal, and who lived with a white person to boot!

Thankfully age and the onset of at least a semblance of good sense has allowed me to dispense with much of that drivel, to see it as foolish at best, dangerous at worst. But Ireland: oh Ireland was different. My admiration for the anti-British revolutionary zeal never dimmed. No matter how atrocious the actions of the Irish Republican Army (IRA) became, my support for the popular refrain 'Give Ireland back to the Irish' compelled me to excuse them. Maybe it was the bog-Irish blood that blunted my Aboriginal facial features or maybe deep down I still nurtured my youthful exuberance; whatever, I was touching down in Northern Ireland and it felt like a homecoming.

This is what I had waited for; I felt like I was at the pinnacle of my career. I allowed myself a moment of satisfaction; it wouldn't get better than this, I told myself. The idea of being a journalist had burned in my mind since I was a boy. Mum tells me I read before

I was four years old, and I have vivid memories of sitting glued to the television watching the latest ABC reports on the Vietnam War. For many years, in fact, I thought the familiar strains of the news theme accompanied the opening titles of a war drama. Now this was the real thing. I'd kicked around and seen some things, reported on the odd violent skirmish and stared into the vacant eyes of my share of corpses. I'd recently covered a crackpot coup in Papua New Guinea, but this, I told myself, this was the big time! Hundreds of years of hatred, I reminded myself. I did the correct thing and tut-tutted about the need for peace, the horrific loss of life, the stupidity of sectarian conflict — but who was I kidding. I wanted a show; in the parlance of the foul trade of journalism, I was there for the 'bang-bang'.

I'd only taken up my position as European correspondent in Channel 7's London bureau about six weeks earlier. It had been a whirlwind introduction to the life of a foreign correspondent. I'd arrived fresh from the Papua New Guinea crisis, put my photos on the desk, organised electricity for my house, then kissed the kids goodbye to see Britain hand over Hong Kong to China. I was back only a day, before packing my bags for Belfast.

It was Tom Cannon's idea that I go. Tom needed to hear the sound of gunfire like proud parents need to hear their children's laughter. It made him feel alive. 'I need an adrenalin rush,' he'd say; God knows his body didn't need it. He wasn't yet twenty-five and had life-threatening deep-vein thrombosis. Despite doctors' warnings he did nothing to alter his lifestyle or his diet; we couldn't go out on a job without stopping for the greasiest serving of takeaway he could find.

By all accounts I shouldn't have liked Tom at all: he was foul-mouthed and bigoted. He didn't read, so I can only wonder where he got his political views from; it was as though he communed with the spirit of Enoch Powell. 'Blacks and Pakis out of England,' he'd say, before adding with no shame, 'Like a good curry, mind.' If he wasn't a cameraman he'd have been a soccer hooligan, but he was a damn good shooter, as we say, and in spite of it all I liked him. I trusted Tom, and in a spot I'd probably let him down before he'd desert me.

Tom loved Irish marching season for the same reason all the media pack loved it: it was exciting. Marching season was a misnomer; it was fighting season. Each year the Protestant Orangemen would dress up, strike up the band and parade down Catholic streets to remind the papists how they whipped them in the Battle of the Boyne three hundred years before. Imagine Turkish immigrants marching down Anzac Parade to celebrate Gallipoli, and you might get the picture. It was an affront to the Catholics. Each year both sides would give lip service to reaching a compromise before embarking on a weekend orgy of violence and destruction.

As I set foot on Irish soil I sniffed the breeze, felt the earth underfoot and tried to imbibe the soul of those rebels I'd known only in my imagination. I wanted to see glamour in the Catholic struggle, I wanted to see pride in their faces and shame in the Protestants'. Every look, every action or movement of the police or military I interpreted as sinister. We drove from the airport to the Europa Hotel in Belfast, the most bombed hotel in all of Europe, gratifying my Hemingway pretensions. Along the road I saw a movement out of the corner of my eye; I dare say the figure in the bushes saw us first, sized us up and decided our fate in the time it takes to blink. The British soldier wriggled back behind the bushes and I shrugged it off with a raised eyebrow and a knowing smirk. Yes, this was occupied territory.

I don't want this to sound like a hoary old journo's war story; I haven't done enough, nor done it well enough, to earn those sorts of bragging rights. But I did travel with a keen eye and I looked for people who resembled my own. I saw in the faces of the Irish Catholics the same faces I had grown up with. They were white, but I understood why they were referred to as 'the blacks of Europe'; they fitted the realpolitik equation of black = powerlessness.

Drumcree was the scene of the first march. It had exploded into a running battle the year before, and the media hovered like vultures around a corpse. The TV crews were lined up along a ridge, while the police in armoured vehicles barricaded the residents in their houses.

This was no ordinary police force; this was a military police force. The locals call them 'black bastards' after the dark uniforms and full-face helmets they wear. The Royal Ulster Constabulary is overwhelmingly Protestant; it explains why they approach their job with such gusto. The Catholic families on this Sunday afternoon were unable to go to church, unable to do their shopping; their children were unable to play in the street. The mood was understandably tense. Local priests mingled with the crowd, supposedly urging calm; but the occasional conspiratorial whisper in the ear of a local tough raised suspicions of a less Christian intent.

In the distance I could hear the pounding of a bass drum and the bleat of bagpipes: the Orangemen. TV crews from the three big American networks — ABC, NBC, CBS — the European broadcasters and the BBC began moving into place. The cameramen — none of whom would have been out of place in a uniform — did the grunt work that journalists too often took credit for. Tom had been here before and he knew the short cuts. He noticed CNN's gun international correspondent Christiaane Amanpour and her crew and we nestled in behind them. My mission was plain: get the best stand-up, a piece to camera, I could manage. From where I sit now I'm dubious about these manipulative devices, but such is the conceit of television that I convinced myself that it would add an air of drama and immediacy to my report.

Tom and I positioned ourselves between the police and the barricaded locals. As the marching band came into view, I began my report: 'As the Orangemen moved out, it was the cue for the police to move in . . .'

My microphone was knocked from my hand by a full bottle of beer. Later, viewing the camera tapes, I would see another bottle come within inches of my right ear. The crowd surged forward — men, women and children — and the police locked into riot formation. I continued: 'Suddenly, it was the sign for all hell to break loose . . .'

A brick hurled through the air struck me on the back. The force knocked me forward. 'Get out of here,' I yelled at Tom, who was still rolling, capturing every moment of my distress on tape. He worked to a simple philosophy: never button off. He shot some great pictures; he also got into a lot of trouble. At that moment safety came before the story. Police fired baton rounds into the crowd; cameramen and journalists scattered. Tom and I found an escape route along a perimeter fence. Blood was trickling down my back and I later discovered I'd chipped a bone; the day was only beginning.

'GET DOWN! GET DOWN!'

The police around us had all dived for cover before I realised why they were shouting at us: we were in the firing line. Tom and I had spent the night filming the running battles that had spilled over on Belfast's streets.

'Belfast is alight to a hundred fires . . .', I'd reported for 'Seven News'. 'The air is thick with smoke and the sound of sirens is matched by the rattle of gunfire.'

We needed images to match the drama of my words. Canny Tom had commandeered a driver for us: a Catholic, but one not ashamed to deny it if need be. In Belfast the situation often called for such life-preserving pragmatism. There's an old joke reporters tell: a journalist is covering a riot when a gun is thrust in his face by a man wearing a balaclava. 'Catholic or Protestant?' he asks. 'Uh, Jewish,' stutters the reporter. Without missing a beat the would-be assassin ups the ante: 'Jewish Catholic or Jewish Protestant?'

Our driver had positioned us between some armoured cars the police had used to cordon off a road. My teenage rebel heart admonished the cowardly reporter I'd become. 'What the hell are you doing here; get over there with the real Irish.' But my instinct for survival told me on this side there was less chance of being asked if I was an Aboriginal Protestant. The Catholics had spent at least an hour hurling Molotov cocktails at the 'black bastards'. Suddenly all went silent, that's when I heard the cops screaming to get down. There was another sound, not easily mistaken for a baton round; a sound that if you didn't hear you were most likely dead.

I checked: I was still alive. I was wedged under an armoured car, my hands over my head. I would like to say I prayed none of the bullets I could hear ricocheting off the vehicle would hit me, but there just wasn't time to think about divine intervention. I'd got myself into this mess; the God I believe in I hope had more justified concerns. Three men in black, balaclavas over their heads, emerged from the shadows and opened fire with AK-47s. As quickly as they appeared they were gone, back to whichever rat-hole on the Falls Road they'd crawled out of. After checking if we were all right, the police jumped to their feet, one of them picking up his helmet to find a bullet had pierced the metal. The very next night in the same spot a policewoman was unlucky enough to be not wearing hers: she was shot dead.

As the police charged, we ran with them. Someone had thrown a bed spring out of a terrace window. It sounds almost comical now, but in the darkness I ran headlong into it, falling heavily. Instinctively I bounced to my feet, no act of bravery, just sheer bloody terror. Fear mixed with adrenalin was a potent anaesthetic: the pain in my back had gone and I didn't notice the blood coming through the rip in my jeans. I didn't catch my breath until Anne Fulwood, the presenter of the news program '11AM', rang for a 'live cross' on the phone. As I spoke to her I could hear the distant echo of gunfire.

TV news is the equivalent of a Chinese meal: it can't be reheated. The next night Tom and I were back on the street looking for the follow-up story. I'd quickly learnt how infuriating Belfast can be for a reporter; one day all you need do is point your camera and you'll find action, the next you can scour the streets and come up empty. It was one of those nights. We chased any whiff of a rumour of action; we drove as far as Londonderry (or Derry, depending on whom you're speaking to), searching for something to build a story on. Refusing to be deterred, Tom eventually stumbled on a fire-fight. We filmed for an hour while police and local kids, none of them over twenty, alternately rushed and retreated. The Catholic boys lobbed firebombs; occasionally gunfire would be heard and returned. We had all the footage we needed and were about to pull out when the police charged again.

They attacked the young rebels, hitting them with batons and kicking them mercilessly when they hit the ground. A group of boys called us over; they urged Tom to film the bloodied face of one of their mates. He'd been brutally bashed and it was difficult to make out his features for the blood. As we made for the car, another group jumped us and tried to wrestle the camera from Tom's grasp.

'Fuck off, fuck off,' Tom screamed. Tom was a big lump of a boy with legs like a premier league striker, but his voice had a habit of jumping a couple of octaves when he got excited. In this moment of desperation, he sounded less than threatening.

'Give us the fecking camera,' the kids yelled, 'give it here or we'll fecking smash it.'

Tom wouldn't budge; he kept wrestling and swearing, the helium in his voice rising. 'Give it to them, Tom,' I urged. We were surrounded by at least a dozen big lads and by my calculation we'd backed an outsider and I'd be content just to get my money back. The gang was concerned that the footage of the beaten boy would be intercepted by British security, thus exposing his identity.

'But we won't use it,' Tom reasoned.

Forget it. The deal was we could leave with the camera but no tapes. They'd been around, these boys, they knew TV crews often switched tapes to protect sensitive material and they searched us for what may have been hidden. I was glad to make it back to the car intact, but there was another surprise in store. As we raced back to the hotel, two men jumped from the bushes at a roundabout and aimed a gun at our car. Our driver noticed that they'd blocked the road with the burnt-out shell of another vehicle; quickly he swerved the car anticlockwise. We escaped, but the car behind us drove straight into the ambush; I have no idea what happened to the occupants.

This was my taste of reality on the streets of Belfast. This, I told myself, was how desperate, angry people behave. Is this what my adolescent revolutionary fetish wished on Australia? There was a noble cause at the core of the Irish troubles, I still believed that. But how many of these street kids throwing Molotov cocktails, hijacking cars and torching buildings were freedom fighters? I didn't see in these thugs the worthy inheritors of Wolfe Tone's vision of a united Ireland.

Two hundred years earlier Tone, a pale, slightly built Dublin barrister, had founded the United Irishmen. Tone was a Protestant, but the Lord mattered less than the land and he had formed what he called a 'brotherhood of affection' with Catholics to throw open the doors of the Protestant-dominated Irish parliament. Fired by the ideas of the French Revolution, Tone convinced the French government to make war on Britain and liberate Ireland. In 1796, Tone stood on the deck of a French ship as it set sail, heading a fleet of thirty-five ships carrying 12 000 men.

The Irish are often cruelly the butt of international jokes, and in December 1796 even Mother Nature decided to have a laugh at their expense. The French flotilla had reached sight of the Irish coast. It had been a remarkably smooth voyage and a new chapter of freedom was about to be written in Ireland's history . . . but the wind turned against them. Day after day the ships were buffeted by squalls of rain and snow; the fleet was slowly being broken up. Tone could see Ireland but he couldn't land. Finally the invasion was aborted and the ships turned back toward France. As Irish historian Thomas Pakenham says, 'It was a Protestant wind.' Two years later, in the great Irish rebellion of 1798, some 30 000 men, women and children were shot down in the space of just two weeks.

This is the history that had sparked my imagination. In my mind the British were the enemy, both in Ireland and in Aboriginal Australia. But I couldn't see glory in Belfast in 1997. The brawlers on the streets had inherited a legacy of violence and hatred, but none of the dignity. Not even my romantic delusions could lift this out of the realm of thuggery.

In another colonised nation fighting for independence, Algeria, Frantz Fanon observed the effect of political and economic domination and concluded that violence begat violence:

> The violence which has ruled over the ordering of the colonial world . . . that same violence will be claimed and taken over by the native at the moment when, deciding to embody history in his own person, he surges into the forbidden quarters.

That's the scientific argument; I tend to favour the view of someone closer to the street, in this case the former chief of staff of the Dublin branch of the IRA during the 1960s, Cathal Goulding. Of his Belfast brothers, Goulding said contemptuously, 'For them the fight had become an end in itself. They were not planning to achieve the freedom of Ireland, they simply wanted to fight for it.'

In the Northern Ireland of the late 1990s, Martin McGuinness was 'the man'. Since the 1970s he and Gerry Adams had been synonymous with the IRA as the leaders of the terrorist organisation's political wing, Sinn Fein. Both, of course, maintain the pretence of denial: 'I am not now, nor ever have been, a member of the IRA.' I even had a chance to put the question directly to McGuinness during an interview when I presented the current affairs program 'Real Life'; I received the standard reply. But the weight of evidence strongly suggests otherwise. Adams always appeared to me a politician, smooth and adept; McGuinness cut a more dangerous figure — aloof, self-contained and with the eyes of the killer many believe he is. McGuinness refuses to be overawed; preparing for a meeting with the Oxbridge-educated British peace negotiators McGuinness said plainly, 'I am Martin McGuinness from Derry, from the bogside' — he could handle any man. McGuinness preached violence; guns, he said, would not be silenced until the British were out of Ireland. 'Without the IRA, we are slaves,' he said. 'We will never be slaves again.'

I had a tenuous but nonetheless personal link with Martin McGuinness. I'd formed a friendship with a Channel 7 producer, Kieren Gill, who'd grown up in Derry and gone to school with Martin. Kieren has an impenetrable Irish brogue and a wary manner which add a conspiratorial air to any conversation. He and I had worked closely on the interview program 'Face to Face' before I left for London. Not long after I met him, Kieren handed me a copy of the IRA handbook and whispered, 'Do you know how to make a bomb out of a cigarette packet?' I laughed; he didn't. You learn these things on the streets of Belfast.

Before I left for London, Kieren slipped me a note. 'If you see Martin, give him this, it'll see you right,' he said. The letter began with the traditional Ulster greeting 'Ahora' and went on to tell McGuinness that this nobody from Australia was okay, 'one of us' so to speak. I got my chance at a rally in a little village outside Belfast. It was the usual scenario: an Orangemen march, police barricades and angry Catholics. McGuinness arrived to pats on the back and cheers from the crowd. He was a folk hero to these people; men wanted to be near him and children wanted to be like him. I had my letter and sensed my opportunity. 'Mr McGuinness, my name's Stan Grant, I'm a reporter from Australia.' Without another word I handed him the letter. I'm surprised he opened it, but he did; a slight smile passed across his lips and he simply looked at me and nodded. I didn't have to ask permission to film for the rest of the day.

I don't know whether McGuinness was present that day to stop trouble or start it. He took off his jacket and jumped up on a fence with a megaphone to plead with the people to stay calm. He was flanked by some of the local boys with the sort of broad backs that made me think they'd stepped off the farm. Then he walked slowly along the line of police, softly taunting them, whispering abuse; just loud enough for them to hear and soft enough to foil our microphones. Suddenly one of the young policemen lashed out with a baton, striking McGuinness on the head; quickly McGuinness turned to the cameras and parted his hair to reveal a deep gash. In an instant he had created the image that would appear on millions of television screens across Great Britain that night. Score one McGuinness.

In the two years I was in London I reported on the ebb and flow of the Irish troubles. I reported on jail break-outs, riots and bashings; I watched films like *The Boxer* and *The General* that kept alive the flicker of romance that still burned in me for Ireland. I also reported the bombing of innocent children in Omagh, and felt sickened and ashamed that I'd ever countenanced violence myself.

Ireland achieved peace on my watch. I was happy but wondered how long it would last, for the history of Ireland tells you that peace simply means time to plot. This was a peace plan brokered by the British Prime Minister, Tony Blair, and the President of the United States, Bill Clinton. I stood outside 10 Downing Street amid a crush of cameras as the terrorists came to the table. Gerry Adams and Martin McGuinness had once been imprisoned as enemies of the state; now in a remarkable twist of history they were sitting down to tea and biscuits with the very people they'd vowed to kill. Gerry Adams was also received at the White House, Clinton making the boldly symbolic gesture of shaking his hand.

There was wild talk at the time of Adams receiving the Nobel Peace Prize. Such was the transformation of a man once photographed next to a wall scrawled with the graffiti slogan: 'The IRA will never be beaten'. Scepticism abounded; a television interviewer questioned Adams's motives only to have the question turned back on himself. 'I've got four bullet holes in my body,' said Adams. 'What have you done for peace?' Is that how we measure commitment, I wondered — in blood?

Australia, I thought, has a violent history, and a great blood debt to Aboriginal people, but Northern Ireland it is not. Australia, for all its shortcomings, grapples with the column of smoke that is justice. Its courts have been used to imprison us, but have also been used to liberate us from the fiction of *terra nullius*. Parliaments have passed laws to deny us our liberty, yet have also spent billions of dollars to make the law work for us. Australian people have looked down on us but have also at times looked up to us, as they did at the Olympic Games.

Perhaps it's all about numbers. If there were enough of us to take back our country maybe we'd pick up the gun too; maybe I'd be the first in line. But that's an argument for teenage fantasy. I don't believe in the Australian myth of egalitarianism, I don't believe in mateship and the 'fair go'. For a black person in Australia, working hard means all you may end up with are blisters and a sore back. 'Hey true blue, it's me and you . . .'; I don't think so. But in that myth there is at least an ideal that binds us in the quest for a shared identity. I looked around Belfast to find people like me; I found people who would just as soon have shot me.

I still believe Ireland should be Irish. The line that separates North from South is like an open wound that will not heal. But sadly so many of the young kids I saw running wild on the streets draw their identity from the blood of that wound. The same goes for the arrogance of the Orangemen, who believe that

Catholics, each year, need a reminder of their powerlessness. My identity as an Aborigine is also drawn from my past. I've deposited the tales of my family's suffering to build up a healthy balance of self-esteem. Like Irish Catholics, I've tried to see hatred in the eyes of my oppressor, but that's no foundation for a future. I am a product of Australia, I don't belong solely to some ancient tribal Aboriginal past, and I certainly do not belong to Ireland.

In 1999 Gerry Adams visited Australia, something that would have been unthinkable only a decade ago. I had returned from London to host Channel 7's evening current affairs program 'Today Tonight'. I kept a keen eye on Irish politics and was desperate to speak with Adams. The organisers of the visit said there would be a news conference, but no individual interviews. I found my seat — front and centre — and proceeded to ask as many questions as I could. As the conference broke up, one of Adams's handlers pulled me aside and told me to wait: 'Gerry would like to meet you.' In a few moments Adams emerged, shook my hand and agreed to an interview. Despite or maybe because of his violent past, I found him easy to speak to and even easier to like. After the interview I told him about myself and my heritage and he seemed as fascinated with the Aboriginal story as I was with the Irish.

'You know,' he said, 'I think of myself as an Irish Aborigine.'

I thought for a moment, then just smiled.

11

History's Orphans

This is what we are, what we civilise ourselves to disguise — the terrifying human animal in us, the exalted, transcendent, self-destructive, untramelled lord of creation. We raise each other to the heights of joy. We tear each other limb from bloody limb.

SALMAN RUSHDIE, *THE FURY*

It's funny how words, uttered innocently, can take on different meanings. I was driving to Tokoza, a wild black township on the outskirts of Johannesburg. My crew and I had organised a black driver, a Zulu, to ferry us to and from these unpredictable places that could explode into violence without warning. My producer, Peter Charley, surveyed the area from the car window.

'That'd be a good place to shoot,' he said.

'Shoot?' replied our driver. 'Yes, very good place for shooting.'

Peter and I looked at each other and broke up laughing. But our friend was serious, deadly serious. He took us to the hostels, dilapidated fibro and tin buildings, where Zulu men stayed while they worked in town. Bullet holes peppered the walls of the buildings, the windowpanes were shattered and the men — young, angry — stared at us blankly, some of them with their arms, chests and legs bandaged from shotgun wounds.

I'd been sent to South Africa to compile a series of stories which would launch the new current affairs program, 'Real Life', that I'd been recruited to anchor for the Seven Network. Apartheid had breathed its last sigh, and in a few weeks Nelson Mandela, a one-time black terrorist jailed for more than a quarter of a century, would become the country's first black president. My stories were to be about hope, about a new multi-racial nation where people would be free to live and love across the colour line. What I found was a people struggling to bury old enmity, a country where the psychological wounds of racial hatred would not heal at the ballot box.

I'd approached the job with some trepidation. Black people in South Africa, and coloured people, as I'd be called, still could not be assured of freedom or equality. I was determined not to be a party to any hint of prejudice or discrimination. I wouldn't humour that country's way of doing business. In Peter I had a kindred spirit, a big barrel-chested man, who loved his job and was good at it. He was a caring man with a conscience; a good man. We demanded a South African film crew that reflected the mix of the nation: an Afrikaner cameraman, a British South African reseacher, and a black sound recordist. We all became firm, lifelong friends as we saw death and terror up close, as we laughed, cried and drank together.

The camaraderie of the road, in my experience, cannot be found anywhere else. We travelled that vast country in a Kombi, we stacked it with beer and sang old Rod Stewart songs at the top of our voices. Our friendship saw no colour, although in quieter moments Milton Nkosi, our black colleague, and I shared stories of pain, his remarkably similar to mine. I left him with an Aboriginal T-shirt I'd worn on the trip and he hugged me and told me we'd always be friends.

Years later in Baghdad, as America prepared to bomb Iraq, I heard a voice behind me at the media centre.

'Does anyone have a spare power point?'

I knew that voice immediately, and as I turned we saw each other and his face beamed.

'Stan!' Milton's laugh and bulging eyes had not changed a bit.

I'd always felt a little guilty about Milton, that somehow I'd let him down. Part of my assignment in South Africa was an interview with the white supremacist leader, Eugene Terre' Blanche. A madman with a massive frame and a deep voice, Terre' Blanche's name meant literally 'white land'. He'd warned of a bloody civil war if Mandela was elected. I'd seen his rallies on television; under a flag eerily similar to Hitler's swastika he would punch the air and froth at the mouth as his supporters cheered his doomsday prophecy. Now I would get to sit down across from him, but under the strict condition that Milton not accompany me.

I'd spoken to Milton about it. I didn't see why we should give in to Terre' Blanche's bigoted demands, but my friend wouldn't budge. He would stay and I would go.

The hot African summer sun had turned my skin a deep, dark brown. I was a lot blacker, I think, than the commander had been led to believe. Terre' Blanche was agitated and speaking quickly in Afrikaans: I didn't understand much of what he said, but I did understand the word 'Kaffir', and I understood it was meant for me. In Australia it'd be 'boong' or 'coon' or 'Abo'; here I was a Kaffir. My cameraman told me later Terre' Blanche had asked who I was and why a Kaffir had been sent to interview him. My crew was smart enough to humour him, and I did the interview . . . with a gun, loaded and placed strategically on his desk, aimed directly at me.

Terre' Blanche was a sideshow, I knew that. He was a man time had passed by, but he spoke for many thousands of white South Africans who refused to accept that blacks could ever be their equals.

Oranja was a town full of such people. All the blacks and coloureds had been kicked out. This little white outpost in the Orange Free State was teaching its children that their future depended on their whiteness. It was there I learnt how ridiculous, how arbitrary, the colour line could be. We passed the local school and I noticed a curly-haired, coffee-coloured girl in the playground.

'I thought there were no blacks here,' I said to our researcher, Tony.

'There aren't,' he said.

'Well, who's that little girl?'

'She's not bl——'

I didn't let Tony finish the sentence; this was absurd. 'What? Are you blind?'

'She can't be black, otherwise she wouldn't be here,' Tony said, with no hint of irony.

I was the one who didn't want to be there. It was a barren place, seemingly deserted with the windows and doors of the houses smashed or hanging off their hinges. This is where bigotry thrives, among people who have no-one beneath them to kick except the dehumanised, disenfranchised blacks.

I'll never forget the look in the eyes of the teacher at the school. They were wide, crazy, possessed. She stared at me, unblinking. The children looked like something out of the film *Village of the Damned*. They sang songs and saluted their flag, dreaming of preserving their white *volkstaat*. Yet on another level everything seemed normal. The teacher, despite her unsettling gaze, was polite, even friendly. Racists often have a way of measuring their words to mask their intent. I could see our story vanishing under the weight of her good manners. Then I got personal.

'What would you do,' I asked, 'if your daughter grew up to marry a black man?'

There was silence; her demeanour changed in an instant, all niceness vanished.

'Well, if she does that she sleeps in her bed as she makes it.' She refused to meet my eyes.

'So you'd have nothing to do with her?' I pressed on.

'That's right.'

I got the message. The interview was over.

As we left town, I asked the driver to pull over so I could interview a man painting his house. He had a thick, almost impenetrable accent and didn't even pretend to be reasonable.

'How would you like it if filthy Kaffirs lived next door?' he said.

'I don't think I'm the person to ask, do you?' I laughed.

'These people are animals; they eat with their hands.'

'What do you think of someone like me?' I asked.

'I feel sorry for you, my friend.'

I felt sorry too: sorry for those people for whom political reform had come too late, like the black workers heading home from Johannesburg to Soweto. Each day they made this ride into terror. I thought Milton was overreacting when he asked Peter and me to hand him our wallets, to remove our watches and jewellery before we boarded what the locals called the death train. No-one looked at anyone else; they kept their eyes down, some clutched Bibles and said hushed prayers. One woman leapt to her feet and began singing loudly. The others joined in, still refusing to lift their eyes.

Only the day before eight people had been hacked to death in a mindless machete attack. Now black soldiers patrolled the platforms which were crisscrossed with barbed wire. Every bump or loud noise choked me with fear. I asked myself why I was doing this. We survived the ride, but many others wouldn't live through our night in Soweto.

The sprawling township was unlike anything I'd expected. I'd known it only on a 48-centimetre television; now it spread before me, a shanty metropolis. The police called it the wild west, and Soweto had a murder rate five times higher than New York at its worst. The human wreckage could be seen strewn along the corridors of the massive Baragwanath Hospital. We saw it, the medicos told us, on a quiet night. Hour after hour a convoy of ambulances ferried the dead and dying. The medical staff were past fatigue and dispensed with the normal hospital routines.

A trail of blood snaked across the floor of the hospital's emergency department. There simply were not enough rooms to keep up with demand. A woman blabbered madly, blood and spit spewing from her mouth while a broken bottle stuck out of her head.

The victims of rape, stabbings and violent bashings, children and the elderly, stretched resources to breaking point. One man was rushed in with a bullet in his chest. The doctors didn't bother preparing surgery, they simply wheeled him into a corner and cut him open, our camera recording every moment. I drank my first beer quickly that night to wash away the taste of blood that had overwhelmed my senses.

All the while I couldn't help thinking how familiar it all was; not the scale of misery, of course, but the sense of hopelessness that simply can't be measured. I've seen it on the faces of anxious mothers and their docile, dying babies in Baghdad, in the pasty, hollowed-out cheeks of Irish Catholic children and in the anti-American braggadocio of Palestinian youths. I've also seen it, far too often, at home in Australia.

Wilcannia could be Tokoza or Alexandra or any one of the many black South African townships I visited. The black people in the dry western New South Wales town had the vote, but it didn't do them much good. They counted themselves Australian citizens, but enjoyed nothing that other Australians took for granted. I'd come to the town because an Aboriginal Legal Service lawyer had warned that if the drinking and drug abuse didn't soon stop, the entire Aboriginal population would be wiped out within a generation.

My blood was there. Among the Aboriginal families in Wilcannia were the Johnsons. My grandmother was a Johnson. They'd been rounded up from Hillston,

Menindee and Carowra Tank at the turn of the century. Like all Aboriginal families, they'd been beaten down and left to eke out a living on repressive reserves or fringe camps around country towns.

I came to Wilcannia not as a cousin, but as a reporter. I'd deliberately stayed clear of Aboriginal stories. I didn't want to be marginalised or seen only as a black reporter. There was another reason: I knew I couldn't be both black and a journalist. Reporters play with other people's lives, we fuss over them, poke and prod them and then move on. We retreat to the safety of our newsrooms or editing suites, and the next day or next week we're in someone else's back yard. Now I was fossicking around in black misery, unaware that I was contributing to the problem.

To tell my viewers about the wretchedness in Wilcannia, I needed to show it. This meant trampling on people's privacy, invading their homes and showing them at their worst. Subterfuge goes hand in hand with sincerity. My black skin opened the doors of the tin humpies and broken-down fibro shacks these people called home. It also let me sit on the black side of the hotel bar. There I could see up close the drinking that the Legal Service lawyer warned would put so many of these Aboriginal kids in early graves.

The two young girls propped up at the bar laughed easily and without inhibition. They threw their heads back and opened their mouths so wide you could see their tonsils vibrate. The more they drank the happier they became. They had a cheekiness, a schoolgirl innocence about them. To me and no doubt to themselves they were indestructible. From the front bar of the main pub in town they could take on the world. They told me they were going to move away, go to the city, get married, have children and make a lot of money. The modest aspirations of city girls were the stuff of dreams for these two. Outside the pub was the grim reality they were chained to — a life of teenage pregnancy, boozing and brawling. This wasn't blackness; this was gut-wrenching poverty. I was black — the girls called me brother — but this life wasn't me.

Other journalists had trodden this path. The former prime minister, Malcolm Fraser, had come to Wilcannia a decade before. He found a people perched on the edge of oblivion. I pulled some of the footage out of the ABC film library. There were pictures of men laughing and playing guitar, singing country music songs and drinking themselves blind. Fraser had gone to Wilcannia to open a new housing project. This was what Australia said we needed: better houses, clean water and good medicine. Now I was standing in the wreckage of hope. The once pristine houses were gone, turned to firewood mostly. Black families lived five or six to a room, the old and young huddled together in makeshift tin shacks that bowed to the elements. I stepped over bodies as men slept off last night's hangovers, oblivious to me or my camera.

This was any Thursday night in any small black town in outback New South Wales. We didn't have to look hard to find our story. We filmed a group of boys — the youngest eight, the oldest not yet in his teens — drinking openly from flagons and beer bottles. We filmed from the shadows as men who could barely see straight swung wild round-arm punches at each other and measured their manhood by how many connected. The two girls I'd shared a drink with just laughed it off. I walked in the graveyard where cheap white crosses passed as headstones. Blacks and whites were divided even in death. You could count up the ages on three black graves and struggle to equal one white life. I spoke to a black health worker who told me of a new problem. She almost whispered her secret. Black men, she said, were molesting their own children.

Fate played Russian roulette with these lives. My father knew this. I'd always thought he was trapped in his wanderlust, living out a modern equivalent of his people's ancient nomadic trails. Now I knew why we moved around so much; why I would count over a dozen changes of school before my teens. We were on the run. My father was trying to outwit the grim reaper I saw on the streets of Wilcannia. He faced off with this malevolent thing called life that sucked the air from your lungs and peeled the flesh from your bones. He looked it in the eye and said, 'You can't take my kids.' I left town convinced I'd done some good. I congratulated myself that people would know at least some small truth of what white Australia had done to my people.

I called my story 'Waiting to Die'. This was the grim prophecy that white settlers had foretold two hundred years before. The night after it aired on the ABC's 'Lateline' program, my phone rang. It was my boss, the head of news and current affairs, Peter Manning, to tell me it was one of the most powerful pieces of television he'd seen. My next phone call was not so complimentary. A black girl from Wilcannia was angry that I'd betrayed her people. She told me that my story had attacked the self-esteem of the Wilcannia blacks, adding to the very problem I'd believed I was exposing. This was the fine line I had to walk. While I was a journalist I was unavoidably on the other side.

I have seen the same unbearable tragedy unfolding in Aboriginal settlements from Moree and Walgett to the Kimberleys in Western Australia. I sat in the dirt with little black kids while they played in the radioactive dust from the Maralinga atomic tests in the 1950s. Sometimes I managed to do some good. I exposed a bungled cleanup of the Maralinga lands, showing how the swirling winds blew the cancerous particles into the tiny settlements that had sprung up along the perimeter of the contaminated ground. I also helped one black woman, who as a young girl had been ripped from her mother's arms, to finally open up about her painful past and confront the very institution, our Australian government, which had allowed this to happen.

* * *

My phone rang, interrupting my quiet Saturday afternoon. I have always hated the sound of the telephone. It's that moment of trepidation, of irrational fear, that the call will change my life in some way, and usually not for the better. I've had phone calls that told me relatives had died. I've been called by my sister, asking me to wire money urgently because my brother was about to be banged up in Goulburn jail. Now the phone was ringing again.

'Hello Stan.' The voice at the other end of the line was unrecognisable for its quiet sobbing.

'. . . Yes,' I said, leaving a pause long enough that it could be interpreted as mild irritation.

'It's Justine Saunders, Stan . . . how dare they do this to us.'

Justine Saunders was a very well-known and accomplished Aboriginal actress. 'They' were the federal government, in particular the Minister for Aboriginal Affairs, Senator John Herron. Herron was a kindly man, a doctor in his life outside parliament, but a hopelessly patronising figure to many black people. Now he'd reopened a lifetime of hurt and anger for Justine by denying that there had ever been a stolen generation.

'We have been kicked in the guts so many times by these people, Stan, and now I want to have my say.' Justine was stifling her tears now and her voice, so muffled before, bristled with intensity.

We talked for at least half an hour while she told the story she'd kept hidden so long. She told me how her childhood had been robbed, as she grew up in uncaring foster homes and in convents with cold, emotionless nuns. She went to sleep each night crying for a loving touch, holding herself as she imagined her mother may have held her. She told me, too, how her mum had walked the streets of Brisbane searching for her Justine, staring into the faces of strangers, hoping to catch a glimpse of that other part of her soul. Justine wanted Australia to know that John Herron was wrong. She'd been stolen, as others had been stolen. Her life could not be reduced to a statistic; her mother's memory deserved better. Justine wanted to tell her story to me. There was more: she wanted me to hand back the Order of Australia she'd once been so proud of, but could no longer believe in.

The stolen generation arouses such passion in Australians. There are many who see it as a gigantic hoax, an attempt by what they sneeringly call the 'Aboriginal industry' to extract an admission of guilt, an apology — and millions of dollars of compensation from the Australian taxpayer. To others it is genocide, the systematic attempt to wipe out a race of people by removing their children and hiding them in white Australia until there were no Aborigines left. The truth, as always, sits uncomfortably somewhere in the middle. But that people suffered, that people still suffer, that Justine and her mum suffered, is undeniable. Politicians, historians and pundits get lost in their exaggerations, handy clichés and dramatic slogans which do nothing but reduce justice to a debate.

I put Justine's story to air. I interviewed Senator Herron, asking him what the point was in arguing whether 10 per cent or 30 per cent of Aboriginal children had been taken from their parents. The government's position was that 10 per cent could not amount to a generation. Surely, I said, a life is a life. I held up Justine's once cherished medal and told him that the next day it would be handed to the governor general, and that Justine would not take it back until the government — the prime minister — said sorry.

I was proud of my story; Justine's story. It's not often in the cutthroat, ratings-driven world of commercial television that I could say I felt good about myself, about our industry. Friends and colleagues called to congratulate me. But the warm feelings vanished with the morning ratings results. How many times had I heard the refrain, 'Abos don't rate'; now I'd hear it again. Later that morning the station manager called a meeting to discuss the 'worrying results'. Around a table we talked about the promotion of the program: could that have been the problem? What about the other stories? Finally my executive producer said what everyone else was thinking.

'We had a lot of complaints and angry phone calls saying you were too hard on the minister, Stan.'

Everyone agreed that we shouldn't ignore stories like this, but maybe we should be a bit more sensitive.

The message I got from this discussion was that 'Abos don't rate, let alone any Abo doing an Abo story'. It reminded me of something else: talking about a problem doesn't solve it. My career may have done wonders for me; I can't say it's made a scrap of difference to how too many Aborigines still live today.

Black Australians, black South Africans, Palestinian kids on the West Bank: they are all victims of the malign influence of history. In the faces of Aboriginal people, I see history's orphans. Their grandparents and their grandparents' parents were overrun by new societies that had little or no use for them.

Tribal societies in Europe had given way to feudalism. Then there'd been the rise of the factories and towns of the industrial revolution. In Australia the old traditions clashed head on with the spread of western capitalism. The old traditions were no defence, and soon gave way to relationships of dependence. Inequalities of class and power were fertile ground for the rise of racism. Aborigines were deemed uncivilised and simply had no currency in this new world.

Now the rich and powerful nations argue about how much they should pay to salve their consciences. Since World War II there's been a growing international trend for restitution and reconciliation. The Marshall Plan accepted the burden of the Allies to rebuild Germany and other European countries. The Germans, in turn, have apologised to and compensated the Jews. The U.S. President, Bill

Clinton, apologised to African-Americans for slavery and to Hawaiians for the conquest of their islands. Queen Elizabeth II has apologised to New Zealand Maoris for the colonisation of their land.

In South Africa, Argentina and Chile commissions of truth and reconciliation have grappled with recognising and paying restitution for injustices in those countries. Canada, North America and New Zealand have built on treaties signed with their indigenous people. In Australia there is still no treaty, the lost children of the policies of removal struggle for recognition in our courts, and in 2004 the federal government still has not said sorry. Instead we talk of reconciliation, and as Elazar Barkan points out in his book *The Guilt of Nations*, reconciliation 'has yet to make a significant difference in the life of poor Aborigines'.

12

Turning Points

Our histories shape our identities.
ELAZAR BARKAN, *THE GUILT OF NATIONS*

It was a cool night on 25 September 2000, when a nation allowed itself to believe it had been transformed in just forty-eight seconds. I sat in the Olympic stadium, watching with a mixture of awe and contempt. Was it churlish not to share in this fantasy? Later I could analyse this, I told myself, see it all as some act of mass delusion, but to scoff then would be disrespectful, like smoking in church. The analogy is not incongruous, for this was a religious event, a liturgy in a sport stadium, complete with its own object of worship: our Lycra-clad Madonna. I traded cynicism for pride, and cried.

I was witnessing a new future, one in which my people could share as equals. No, not equals, more than that: we were special. This is what we had fought for; in Sydney's Olympic stadium we could tell ourselves we had found justice. Yet there in our moment of greatest public acclaim was also the greatest challenge to our identity. Success and blackness are strangers, they fight each other for our souls. Now I had to ask myself whether our sense of pride and self-esteem, our identity, was so malleable, so tenuous, that it could be redefined by something as illusory as an Olympic gold medal.

There in front of our eyes we had a black person for our age: Cathy Freeman. She was a touchstone, but amorphous. Cathy could be whatever we wanted her to be. Writers searched for metaphors and thumbed their thesauruses to capture her transcendence. The journalist Bruce Wilson mythologised Cathy as the embodiment of Australian spirit. She was, wrote Wilson, in Sydney's *Daily Telegraph*, the embodiment of 'all things we hold dear: guts, and the will to win for her country'. Even the normally parochial Americans were moved, seeing in Freeman not a slight, black runner, but a social redeemer. The *Washington Post* sports columnist Michael Wilbon wrote:

> In less than 50 seconds she had become an Olympic champion, given Aboriginal people unprecedented public triumph, endeared herself to mainstream Australia and catalysed the process to reconcile the two.

Cathy's win was immortalised, lifted from the realm of ordinary achievement and placed on the pantheon of destiny. Her destiny and the destiny of a nation were inseparable.

The Sydney Olympics was a spiritual revival, one which rendered denominations obsolete, that dispensed with dogma. Even atheists and agnostics were at home in this broad church of Australian sport. This was a unique Australian syncretism, drawn equally from Sidney Nolan and Banjo Paterson, Albert Namatjira and Oodgeroo Noonuccal. It canonised both Paul Hogan and Ernie Dingo. We were creating ourselves in our own image. Before the world we christened this new child 'Australia'; not with a discreet daub of water on the forehead but a full immersion, pronouncing ourselves cleansed of our nation's bloody origins.

What more potent image could we have conjured up than the powerful figure of Aboriginal dancer Djakapurra Munyarryun, representing our dark past, leading little fair-haired Nikki Webster by the hand into our bright new future. We told the world that we had indeed finally prepared a place at our table for Aborigines. No longer were they black plaster figures nestled alongside ceramic gnomes at the bottom of the garden; they were liberated from the flora and fauna and set centre stage as icons of Australia's new image as a timeless land with an exotic past.

And there I was, at once a part of this and yet feeling strangely separate. I knew that to embrace this moment was also to surrender, to lay to rest the generations of hurt that was my family's inheritance. Where was my grandfather Keith in this? What of Aunty Eunice and great-great grandfather Frank Foster? Is this what Wiindhuraydhine and Wongamar could have imagined for me, for their people? If this was a religious ceremony then I, too, had a confession to make. Like this nation I had to make sense of my history, the choices I'd made, the people I'd loved and left. I had to understand my anger and my shame. Especially my shame.

I had stood at another moment in history, much like this, once before. Almost a decade earlier I had called the prime minister, Paul Keating, to a stage in Redfern where he would plunge a knife into the heart of Australian history. He would bleed over its pages and ask us — the Aboriginal people — to forgive, and he would make a pledge to turn pain into hope:

> Isn't it reasonable to say that if we can build a prosperous and remarkably harmonious multicultural society in Australia, surely we can find just solutions to the problems which beset the first Australians . . . It begins with a recognition. Recognition that it was us who did the dispossessing.

This was Keating at his eloquent best. On 10 December 1992, International Human Rights Day, he strode to the podium, the summer sunshine catching the glint in his eye as I introduced him to the mostly black crowd. He was about to deliver a speech that would be the apotheosis of the 'new history', the history that shattered 'the great Australian silence', that told of invasion, bloodshed and prejudice, a history later derided by critics, including Keating's prime ministerial successor, John Howard, as a 'black armband'. Keating's words resonated with Aborigines seeking validation, empathy, and with an Australia increasingly anxious to settle its account with its past, a past many felt cast a pall over their future.

I had observed Keating up close for years. As a young political correspondent with the ABC, I watched him dominate parliament. In the House he was a commanding figure; he strode it like a street tough marking his turf, he was a scrapper who used language like a knuckle-duster. Yet his set speeches were often strangely devoid of fire and passion. On that December day the words written on the page challenged his delivery to match their meaning. Slowly the crowd hushed, sensing the weight of the moment. I caught the eye of Sol Bellear, another Aborigine sharing the stage that day. Simultaneously we raised our eyebrows and nodded as much in surprise as agreement.

'We took the traditional lands and smashed a traditional way of life,' Keating said, 'we brought the disease, the alcohol; we committed the murders; we took the children from their mothers; we practised discrimination and exclusion; it was our ignorance and our prejudice.'

I have a copy of that speech, known as 'the Redfern Park Statement', on my wall at home. It's signed by Paul Keating, a memento of my front-row seat at history. At times I have looked on it as the equivalent of the American Declaration of Independence or Lincoln's Gettysburg Address. Like those epochal commitments, this was the defining moment of a new nation with a new sense of itself. Reconciliation was real, as unavoidable as death and taxes; we could debate how much we owed, we could try to put it off, but from that day on we could not ignore it. Keating concluded his statement with a plea: we must make amends.

'We cannot imagine that we will fail,' he said, 'and with the spirit that is here today I am confident that we won't. I am confident that we will succeed in this decade.'

Cathy Freeman was not yet twenty, and still with stars in her eyes from the Barcelona Olympics, but those words from Keating had just framed her destiny.

Keating's landmark statement would never have occured had it not been for the High Court's Mabo decision, which finally overturned the legal fiction of *terra nullius*, and recognised native title. Now we Aborigines had proof we were robbed. Justices Deane and Gaudron said as much; writing their judgment in the margin that separates mere law from the higher ideal of justice, they characterised dispossession as a 'national legacy of unutterable shame'. 'The nation as a whole must remain diminished,' they wrote, 'unless and until there is an acknowledgment of and a retreat from those past injustices.'

Keating seized on the judgment as the catalyst for a 'new relationship between Indigenous and non-

Aboriginal Australians'. Mabo was more than a legal watershed, it punctured the conservative history of Australia as founded on peaceful settlement. The core of Australian identity had always excluded Aborigines; we were deemed to exist in an archaic age and Australia was a modern nation of modern people. The price of entry to Australia was the disavowal of culture and colour, even family. Now the graves of the past had been opened and bullet holes found in the skeletons. The old Australian was sentenced to death and entombed with his once unshakeable convictions. As his conservative sons paid their respects they knew they could no longer hoard their inheritance; a bastard child had usurped the family and they would need a compelling argument to deny him. Others determined to 'let the dead bury the dead', and composed a future bathed in the light of justice.

The uncertainty in Australia was mirrored by a growing international dislocation. Economically we were no longer a farm and a quarry, and as a people we were no longer 'white'. Our place in the world was more tenuous. Historian Bain Attwood has argued in his book *In the Age of Mabo* that globalism and the increasing homogeneity of world culture saw Australians mine the wealth of Aboriginal culture and heritage for a sense of difference:

> In searching for markers of the cultural difference required to differentiate Australia from other

> nations, the nation-state can no longer utlilise many of those which it has relied upon traditionally — whiteness or more particularly Britishness . . .

For Aborigines there was danger in this. To counter our challenge to their legitimacy, white Australians were appropriating our symbols, our imagery, indeed our identity. To ease the nation's 'unutterable shame' risked, for blacks, a second dispossession: a dispossession of our life-affirming history. We were witnessing a celebration of survival that also threatened to end it. Paul Keating's speechwriter, Don Watson, measured his words for full effect: we were no longer Aborigines but 'Indigenous Australians', or the 'first Australians'. This linguistic sleight of hand masked a quantum leap in historiography. From the moment the British flag was raised on this soil, we became 'Aborigines'. The new settlers became the Australians, we became the blacks. The Afro-American writer Manning Marable, in *Beyond Black and White*, identifies a similar process in the United States:

> Blackness in a racially stratified society is always the 'negation of whiteness'. To be white is not a sign of culture, or a statement of biology or genetics: it is essentially a power relationship, a statement of authority, a social construct which is perpetuated by systems of privilege, the consolidation of property and status.

Aborigines had never been 'Australians': Australians were white. To be an Aborigine, a blackfella, was to be on the losing end; now we were being told we were winners. It was confusing. All around us, the message was growing louder: the Aboriginal past is Australia's future. We saw it on tourist brochures of Uluru and Kakadu; we saw it on television commercials. Whites 'still called Australia home'; the High Court had recognised it had always been ours. White Australians sang along with blacks to the Yothu Yindi song 'Treaty', neither, arguably, knowing what it meant. Actor–comedian Paul Hogan even created a 'white Aborigine' and named him Crocodile Dundee. Yes, we could 'win' and what's more we had a winner: Cathy Freeman.

Now here I was in the Olympic stadium, watching someone I liked to call my friend achieve her dream and that of her Australian nation. It was happening at the close of the decade, as Paul Keating had prophesied in 1992. Of course I was pleased for her. I had interviewed Cathy many times, and each time we greeted each other with a hug and kiss, an embrace of kinship. Our families, we sensed, shared the same pain. Our blackness was the fulcrum of our identity, a mutual acknowledgment. Not based on a problematic preponderance of Aboriginal blood, but a nod to our common past which bound our future. After she won her first world title at Athens in 1997, we sat in a little café eating pizza, drinking beer and reminiscing about the country and western songs our fathers had raised us on. Marty Robbins's 'El Paso' was her favourite, a maudlin tale of unrequited love which ends in tragedy.

But we'd transcended the fatalism of those songs that were the mournful soundtrack of the pallid lives of countless of our countrymen. Cathy the triumphant Olympian; me, a face known to hundreds of thousands of television viewers. Were we to find our place in this new Australia? Would it include our less fortunate brothers and sisters? Would the young faces around me that night in the Olympic stadium, proudly clutching their black, red and yellow flags, deliver the just future for their nation their parents and grandparents had failed to achieve?

I wonder Evonne, when you're playing straight
sets;
And you 'haste' your opponent so well,
Do you ever look back at your grandmother, black;
And catch a glimpse of her in her hell.

Aboriginal poet Kevin Gilbert had written that for our cousin Evonne Goolagong, when she was at the height of her fame. I pondered the words and found resonance not just for Cathy but for me. Does success demand that we forfeit our past? Do we conveniently turn a blind eye to suffering? Somewhere between Paul Keating's Redfern statement and Cathy's Olympic glory lay our past and our future.

Inside the adult lives the child whose dreams draw us back into ourselves; whose innocent eyes, if we let them, allow us to glimpse truth and judge ourselves free of adult conceit and ego. My child lives in me still, he's my refuge from my often melancholy nature. So much of my life is measured in the fragments of memory: of places and people, of days and months and years that slowly have shaped the person I've become. I can stand apart from my past now, as though I'm looking in on someone else entirely.

At times I've wondered if my life has been a dream. Perhaps I'll wake and find myself in the small two-room house in the bed I shared with my brothers, my grandfather sleeping near the fire in the front room. It's where I left myself, where time left the little boy and the galloping years took my youth. There's something back there, in the life not yet lived, that speaks to me of truth and simplicity. There, I walked to school in other people's cast-off clothes. There, I would wait outside the pub to help my grandfather home, and with my mum's note in hand head off to do the shopping, proud that I would return with every cent accounted for. There, there was no waste: no time, money or food to spill. The memory of those days fills me still with warmth; it's what I've spent a lifetime searching for as I've filled each passing year with more detail, more complications.

As I said, my years are marked by fragments of memory. We moved so often that all I can recall are smells, sights and sounds. There's my father playing Duane Eddy guitar licks — 'Rebel Rouser' and 'Forty Miles of Bad Road' — my uncle singing Roy Orbison's

'Pretty Woman', and my aunty dancing in the back room to Petula Clarke and Sandy Shaw. There's my mother doing the ironing and watching 'Coronation Street', and the smell of the mince and onions she'd stretch into a meal. I can still taste Vienna Chocolate ice creams and hot chips on the way home from footy training. I remember the deep, bittersweet taste of my grandfather's dark Club chocolate. I remember the smell of my new baby brother, Glen, after I trudged up the hill to the hospital in Merriwa.

Money was in short supply and to be savoured. There was no budgeting; whatever we had we spent. Any windfall was an excuse for takeaway food, or a meal at a cafe, or the movies. I spent my childhood with my eyes fixed to the ground in a search for loose change, or checking for uncollected coins in the phone box. I remember once finding twenty-five cents embedded in a freshly tarred road. My grandfather and I sharpened old paddle pop sticks and chiselled away until we'd freed the money and headed for the nearest lolly shop. Poverty bred ingenuity. My father would walk the streets looking for half-smoked cigarette bumpers and carefully note their location, then he'd cajole Mum into collecting them, his habit satisfied and his pride intact.

My father worked in sawmills mostly; back-breaking, lung-busting work. Occasionally he'd hit on a get-rich-quick scheme, like the time he turned fruit vendor. Dad had bought a truck and decided to load it with fruit and vegetables and hawk them from town to town. I excused myself from school — my education was sporadic to say the least — and hit the road. Twenty cents a bucket, I'd run up and down the streets, knocking door to door on the promise of a two-cent commission on each bucket off-loaded. Neither of us got rich, and it wasn't long before Dad was back on the mills and we were on the move to another dusty little town. Such was the pattern of my childhood, a succession of towns, shacks and schools, but always there was a dream, a faint hope that one day I might become a journalist. I carried my ambition for as long as I can remember. I didn't speak too often about my dream, I just quietly nurtured it not knowing how or if it would ever come true.

Then we moved to Canberra. Canberra was my turning point. For once my family stayed in one place long enough for me to go to school uninterrupted. And Canberra was a hotbed of Aboriginal political activity. Slowly, I absorbed it, realising that my options were not limited, that for an Aborigine with an education life promised more than dusty towns, loose change and sawmills. Marcia Langton helped open my eyes. Now she's Professor Marcia Langton, renowned anthropologist and historian, then she was a young beautiful black firebrand with piercing eyes; she was angry but had resolved to fight with her mind. Marcia made me realise that a black boy could dream, and more than that, that my dream could become real. I'd met Marcia while working part time at the Australian Institute of Aboriginal and Torres

Strait Islander Studies; it was there in the library that she sat me down and told me I had choices, I didn't have to be a victim. By the end of our discussion she had me all but enrolled at the University of New South Wales; within months I was indeed sitting in the lecture hall learning politics from Professor Donald Horne and sociology from Sol Encel.

Twenty years have passed since then; twenty years with their own memories, marking the journey of the boy I was to the man I have become. Fortune has favoured me when my instincts would have let me down. The doors of journalism opened as if preordained. Tony Bartlett saw enough in me to offer me a cadetship with the Macquarie Radio network. From there it was to the ABC and four years in the federal parliamentary press gallery. There I worked and learnt from the best: Jim Middleton, Russell Barton, Paul Lyneham and Kerry O'Brien, all of them generous in their support and encouragement. Journalism has been good to me. I have travelled the world, interviewed prime ministers and presidents, I have had the opportunity to talk to millions of Australians as host of my own news and current affairs programs. I have lived well and my hands have softened with comfort. Not for me the fate of my father, who looks on my career and life with both pride and bewilderment at a world he could never really know. The years have taken me from him in very many ways, from my family and the certainty of life as an Aborigine, however harsh that may be.

The price of my success has too often been paid by others. The life I've chosen, or perhaps fate has prepared for me, has been a selfish one. Through it all was the woman I called my wife, a woman who blessed me with three beautiful children. How do I even begin to make sense of this love that simply ran out? How is it that the years we shared, the joy and tenderness, could take us apart, not draw us together? Karla and I met before we were out of our teens. We were children, in love and linked by our Aboriginal culture. We dreamed and took each step together. Karla made sacrifices and I gladly accepted them.

We were still so young when our baby was born. Karla cried when she told me she was pregnant and I promised her I would never let her down. Lowanna, our little girl, came slowly and was so tiny, and I held her trying to feel like a father.

Karla and I made the promises of youth, and for many years we kept them. The end of a marriage can sour the memories; where once was love is all too often bitterness. Not for me. The failings were more mine than hers. We would fall apart and somehow patch things up and find shelter in each other again. Our years shone, but as Karla and I met as children we left each other as a man and a woman. The years had turned love to fondness and that didn't do us justice. Our conversations had become like stocktaking. There was a future for us, but not together. Yet our childhood love created immortality with our three beautiful babies, Lowanna, John and Dylan.

So here was my confession. As I watched the Olympic opening ceremony, this was the sum total of my life. As a nation we were wrestling with our past, searching for an identity that included us all; as an Aborigine and a man I was doing the same. Like Cathy Freeman, I, with thousands of other Aboriginal people, was on the verge of a new time; we were being told that history could be righted, that the pain of our ancestors would not be our burden.

As Cathy beamed with joy on the winners' dais, her face illuminated by the flashes of a hundred thousand cameras, another story was being told just outside the stadium gates. The Aboriginal display at the Olympic Expo was sticking doggedly to a far more confronting picture, a tale of human tragedy less easily mythologised than a foot race. A thoughtful international visitor would have found it difficult to reconcile such an overwhelming display of unity with a history of race relations marked by violence, apathy and abuse. A casual glance at the expo would have left our visitor with an image of a people stripped of their dignity, denied their humanity, dispossessed, disenfranchised, their liberty taken from them, their children removed from their love and care. 'We're doing fine in the lucky country,' white Australia seemed to say, while the pitiful black reality screamed, 'Poor bugger me!'

Assimilation was a moot point, at least for me. I sat in the stands with my new white partner, her mum and her mum's boyfriend, a Maori. We all cheered for Cathy; for Australia. Around me were children, mostly white, but some Vietnamese, Lebanese, Greek or Italian, so many of them waving the red, black and yellow flag we once saw as peculiarly Aboriginal. Once it flew truly as a symbol of defiance; now, like Cathy, it spoke of unity.

For whom did Cathy run? I think of my grandfather, Keith Cameron, arrested from his bed and tied to a tree, left all day in the blazing sun because a policeman suspected he had been drinking. Did she run for him or for the descendants of the cop who tied him up? More personally, did she run for her grandmother Alice who was taken as a child from her family? Did she run for the prime minister, John Howard, who refused to apologise for her family's pain? My grandfather, Cathy's grandmother: they are our personal life-support systems connecting us to a past where our sense of Aboriginality lies. Black people are rooted in the past, it defines us.

'Coz I'm free'. Cathy has the words tattooed on her shoulder. Free of what? Free of her historical past; free of the shame she felt as a black child; free of the fate of her grandmother Alice; free to pledge allegiance to Australia's history. Aborigines had no history other than that written by the colonisers. History is written by winners; our forebears had been cast as losers. Scavenging in the junkyard of our collective memory we'd perversely drawn nourishment from our plight. Freedom has been our struggle as much as our destination. My ancestors, my family, had delivered me to this moment in history; as my country embraced a new future, so did I. As an Aborigine and a man, I had in so many ways outgrown my past.

13

My Traitor's Heart

. . . each of us, helplessly and forever, contains the other — male in female, female in male, white in black and black in white. We are a part of each other.

JAMES BALDWIN

I know a place where evil killed time. There, fathers were fated never again to look on their children; sons would never become fathers. They were sent to God in a furnace of hell. There, the time-blackened heads and hands of saints are preserved in glass jars. I lit a candle and said a prayer for the dead, and I fell in love.

The clock above the church in the tiny Greek village of Kalavryta stopped, never to start again, the day Hitler's robotic henchmen set fire to the town's soul. All of the men — grandfathers, their sons, and their sons' sons — were rounded up and forced into the church, the door locked. The German soldiers set fire to the building, trapping the screams of their tortured victims forever inside. The women, too, were crowded into a tiny schoolhouse with equally murderous intent. But the God these people believed in miraculously worked his mercy. A German officer defied his orders and listened for a moment to his conscience. He left the door of the schoolhouse ajar, offering the women their chance at survival.

A white cross stands on the hill overlooking the village, casting its shadowy reminder of the horror that visited and remains embedded in the memory of those who live there still. Men now sit again in the town square, they sip coffee and stare out through the eyes of interlopers. They're not from here, they know that, yet they've come to lend their seed and restore the natural order of things. Young boys play with girls and the old women look on, seeing hope's dream realised.

I came here by accident. The Olympic torch had begun wending its way from its ancient home of Olympia to its destination at the 2000 Olympic Games in Sydney. Unexpectedly, I was sent to broadcast the lighting of the flame, the eternal harbinger of peace. I was in Kalavryta, where the locals had come out to welcome the runner who'd brought this symbol of humanity. These people worshipped it, they truly knew its value more than most.

My head was pounding. The blossoms of spring were burning my nose and the back of my throat with a ferocity that made my eyes water. I wanted desperately to feel the power of this place, but my senses were battered by my allergy to pollen. My colleague Tracey Holmes was in the crowd with the television crew recording her story. Tracey and I barely knew each other when we were sent to Greece to work together. Daily, my respect for her talent and professionalism grew. There was more. I sensed a much deeper attraction; one that I could not ignore, no matter how much I tried. We shared talks and walks and I met a gentle soul, a lover of life, colour and beauty. I watched her when she wasn't looking and later I discovered she did the same with me.

Love doesn't seek permission, it poses more questions than it answers. I wasn't ready for this; Tracey wasn't ready.

We walked through the narrow backstreets of the village, trying to find a chemist where I could get some relief. Trying to make ourselves understood, we laughed and I continued sneezing. We did find some medication, but we found something much, much more; we found each other. We drove that day from Kalavryta to Athens, the chiming bells around the necks of mountain goats echoing through the hills; it's a sound I hear now when I remember that place, a place of death, a place of peace and a place of love.

We can block our ears to love's call and bury our regret with the consolation that we did our duty — or we can say yes! Yes to joy and to heartache, yes to fear and uncertainty. I had no right to this love; my wife and my children had their claims on my heart. I still can't say that I deserve my happiness at the expense of others. I will mark each day with a silent tear for my other life lost. But I had grown hard; I had armed myself with a sword for too long, and I wanted to put it down for a harp. I knew only that I wanted to hear music again.

This felt like the love I'd read about in myths. This love called me into a forest and asked me to enter at its darkest point. There was no trail for me to follow, and no guide, guru or companion to light my path. Love makes us truly alone; the ancient tales tell us that we must know ourselves — slay our dragons — before we can truly know another. My shattered taboos were not just moral, but racial. In Tracey I had found a soulmate, but one who belonged to a world which had shunned my family and which I had resolved never really to be part of. But if I could love a white person, I knew also that I could never again hate one.

I had always deeply mistrusted those blacks who were married to whites. In my mind they'd sold out; their love — if love it was — was treasonous. So often it was the most successful Aborigines, almost always men, who claimed a white partner for a trophy. They doth protest too much, I thought. They were the first to scream racism and they spoke of black pride, all the while lying down with whites and breeding children who were more white than black.

I had sought security in my identity. My wife was an Aboriginal woman, proud of her heritage. Our children had no divided loyalties. I had never contemplated it any other way. I had to live and work in white Australia, but my heart would never truly be Australian. Now it had all unravelled so quickly. I was undone. Exposed. I betrayed not only my marriage but — in my mind at least — my race.

Tracey didn't escape censure either. She had lived the life of a gypsy. Her parents were surfers who'd lived in South Africa and Hawaii and had an easy rapport with black people. Tracey had a naive but endearing attitude to colour: she simply refused to see it. Others, though, who came under the guise of friendship, brought her a warning: stay away from Stan. Yes, they conceded, I was nice enough, I'd worked hard and been successful, but, they added, 'They're different, you know.'

Different. A vague message, but pointed enough to let Tracey know it would never work. There's a challenge in mixed relationships that strikes at the very heart of Australia's primal instincts on race. We half-castes were history's shame. We were the living proof of the lie of Australian settlement. Could Aborigines really be savages, near brutes, with no legal claim to this land if the brave white settlers would sleep with us? Australia convinced itself we were the product of lust not love; love existed between white people, love existed between human beings.

I've never wanted to let Australia off the hook. Even if I carried my resentment well hidden, masked with a smile, I could comfort myself that I'd refused to cede my soul. I have despised Australia at times for stealing my sense of wonder and condemning me to look at the world through the eyes of a cynic. I could never truly believe in the Anzacs; Australia Day, I convinced myself, was a time of mourning not celebration. As a child I repeated the oath of allegiance and saluted the flag with my fingers crossed behind my back. I have revelled in cheap revenge; cheering on the All Blacks against the Wallabies and rejoicing as each Aussie wicket fell against the might of the West Indies cricket team.

I have always known too much, been too suspicious, too mistrustful, to feel at peace here. The white blood in my veins made me reject Australia all the more, because I knew the price my family had paid for our whiteness. I have grown to be wary of the meanness, the nastiness, the viciousness I've seen at the core of the Australian character. White Australia, it's always seemed to me, was not so much a policy as a prophecy. For two centuries this European outpost has been cut off from its colour, threatened by the 'yellow peril' that surrounds it and the blackness that has pulsed at this continent's heart for two thousand generations. Like so many of my people, I had nursed a deeply wounded psyche. Now I asked myself if my identity was not as fickle as love.

His tiny hand fits comfortably into my palm. It's soft, untouched by the hardness of the world. It's so delicate and so white. Against his, my skin takes on an even deeper copper hue. He's only just learning to reach out to me, to look up and see in my eyes something of himself. He needs me. I have made him; my blood is his blood. I need him too. I need the unconditional love of his smile. He's my son. He's my Jesse.

A shoot will come up from the stump of Jesse;
from his roots a Branch will bear fruit.
The spirit of the Lord will rest on him —
the spirit of wisdom and of understanding,
the spirit of counsel and of power,
and of the fear of the Lord —
and he will delight in the fear of the Lord.

He will not judge by what he sees with his eyes,
or decide by what he hears with his ears;
but with righteousness he will judge the needy,
with justice he will give decisions for the poor of the earth.
He will strike the earth with the rod of his mouth;
with the breath of his lips he will slay the wicked.
Righteousness will be his belt
and faithfulness the sash around his waist.

The wolf will live with the lamb,
the leopard will lie down with the goat,
the calf and lion and the yearling together;
and a little child will lead them.
(Isaiah 11:1–6)

For nearly thirty hours our unborn baby had wreaked havoc on his mother. With each contraction he'd threatened to come into the world, but something in him clung to the womb. Through a haze of morphine and pain-numbing gas, Tracey continued to bear down. She vomited and rested and vomited again. The midwives placed her on a drip, and still her cervix refused to dilate. I'd watched it all with a sense of helplessness, as all expectant fathers must. I felt like the powerless witness to a slow-moving car crash. Unable to ease Tracey's pain, I blamed myself. There's too much of the mission blackfella in me; if something's wrong, I must be the cause.

I thought of the arguments we'd had. I felt shame at the abuse I'd hurled at her. There were times I'd wished our baby would never be born. Tracey and I had been together only a year, and not a day of it had been easy. Our lives were gossip fodder, we were scrutinised and criticised, and we struggled with the pain our love had caused others who loved us. And I was black; and I would never let her forget it.

It wasn't her whiteness we fought over, it was my blackness. Tracey just wasn't as attached to her colour as I was to mine. We'd raise our voices and I'd fight from the trenches of colour. Tracey was white. Worse, she was a racist, I'd yell. Worse again, her family, her friends, were racist. Worse still, the baby she carried — my baby — was white too. It was an uncontrollable, reflexive hatred. It came from that scar on my soul, that part of me that expected, even provoked rejection. It came from not ever feeling good enough. The truth is that Tracey wasn't the racist — I was.

I was being punished. I'd willed my baby not to be born and now he wouldn't. The obstetrician decided on a Caesarean delivery. Tracey had battled too long, she'd gone past exhaustion and only a mother's instinct for survival remained. Of course these procedures were commonplace, and the risk to mother and child was minimal. I reassured myself of that, over and over, as I went outside for some air. Guilt wouldn't let me go; somehow on some level I couldn't escape the feeling that this was my fault. I sat down and wrote a letter to Tracey; I wanted her to know how much I loved her and that I so wanted our baby.

> Trace, I want him to know he is safe in my arms. I want him to feel the love of his brothers and sister. Most of all I want him to know his mum.
>
> Like you, our Jesse has no colour; he is the beauty of the rainbow, a crystal to hold up to the light and reflect love.
>
> Have our baby, Trace. I am so proud of you.
>
> Love always
>
> Stan

We chose our baby's name carefully, Tracey and I. Jesse came from the Old Testament book of Isaiah; to Jesse we have added Martin — after Dr Martin Luther King junior — and Justice. He's born out of our love and our commitment to each other. But more than that he is a new beginning; our own belief in what this country can be. My children are my investment in hope.

Jesse is my youngest and he's blessed with two strong brothers and a beautiful sister. Lowanna, my daughter, is named after an Aboriginal word for beauty; John is little John of God; and Dylan, my golden-haired, blue-eyed boy, has the name my father gave to me. We can never be the parents our children deserve. I've failed my first three babies in ways I will always regret, and my little boy Jesse, too, I hope, will learn to forgive his dad.

My children inherit this country's legacy. My history, my family's history, has made them. The blood debt, the price of pain, has been paid in full. The courage and love of their ancestors, I hope, will spare my children this nation's harsh judgment. Once, not so long ago, they would have been condemned by their blackness; now they can be proud of their heritage. For Jesse there's also his mum's story; a story that meets mine and in him writes its own page.

As ever we're the small lives, the backdrop to the main players on Australia's stage. There are big questions — so many seemingly unanswerable questions — that bedevil us still. Feminist and academic Germaine Greer has called it our unresolved blackness. She says Australia will never be at peace until it embraces the truth of its Aboriginality. Yet the story of my people, my own family, a black family, shows it's not that simple. Our search has been as much to reconcile our whiteness as it has been to hang on to the black in us.

* * *

'Hi Stan, it's Peter Ford.'

Peter had been a friend and colleague back in Australia; now on National Sorry Day he wanted me to know that his thoughts were with me and my family. His voice so far away, so heartfelt, made me think of my mother and father, my grandparents and great-grandparents. I thought of their suffering and their dignity and their love.

'Thank you Peter,' I said.

There was nothing else for me to say; nothing he could add. 'Sorry' said it all. There was no need even for goodbyes; I shut off the phone, stood in the middle of London and quietly cried.

Epilogue

My people believe in the power of dreams. In dreams we become whole; in dreams we become men. My father came to me in a dream, he came from half a world away and he came to tell me it was all right; whatever had happened and whatever would happen, it was all right.

In my dream Dad was walking toward me, flanked by two of his cousins, my uncles, and they were on the stairs of an old railway platform. There was no-one else around and I was in a time that belonged to neither day nor night. They seemed not to notice me. As they got closer I saw they wore no shoes. It seemed odd. Then, like spirits, they glided past me. Dad paused only to whisper in my ear, 'At least I don't make excuses for what I've done.'

I woke the next morning with my memory of the dream as clear as if they'd been in the room with me. My father's message kept replaying over and over in my mind, each time sounding more ominous. It was like a grim prophecy and I was condemned to its fulfilment. At that moment I was as far from Dad as I'd ever been. I was the Seven Network's correspondent in London, preparing news reports for broadcast by satellite back to Australia each night. But my father had no need of satellites; his technology was more ancient, yet he came to me as clearly as I'd ever appeared on screen.

For two thousand generations my father's people, the Wiradjuri, had believed in the power of our dreams. The old men, the Walamira, had a psychic gift that enabled them to thrust their minds into the future, into a spirit world where distance, time and space dissolved.

The Walamira were the keepers of our secrets. They had the power of flight and the power of illusion, and they possessed an impenetrable intellect. They could be identified by the light in their eyes and they spoke directly to Baiami — to God. Baiami would take young boys in their dreams and ask them if they'd been prepared by their fathers to receive the ancient power and knowledge. Then he would promise to make them men. My father had come to ask me if I was ready to become a man.

Am I ready to become a man? An Aboriginal man? To answer that question I've had to ask other, even more searching questions. Where do I belong? Who am I? The blood of my fathers links me to a much older place and time. I've walked in the footprints of my ancestors; I've sat by the riverbank at night and imagined them around me. I am all that they have made me. Yet I stand apart from them now. I call myself an Aborigine. I know I am from them, but am I still truly of them? James Baldwin said of the modern black American facing his African counterpart:

> An American Negro, however deep his sympathies or however bright his rage, ceases to be simply a black man when he faces a black man from Africa.

Aboriginal identity has become too often bound up in sentiment and self-righteousness. It's too often simply convenient. It can wither under too intense a gaze. So too that must be true of me looking into the eyes of many of my black countrymen. Success, or acceptance, has come at a cost to the certainty of my identity. But it can be no other way; to choose otherwise would be to shy away from the arguably meagre yet hard-won freedom my parents have struggled and sacrificed for. This dilemma will confront so many of my brothers and sisters as they too grapple with how to express themselves in a world imposed upon them, which is at the same time tempting, seductive. White Australia engulfs us; we fight for its concession, while it sets the limits of our existence and daily defines us.

Aboriginal identify, then, is the most fragile, brittle of possessions. Blond hair, blue eyes, a straight nose, or just as easily a good car, a nice house, an education, can shake a so-called Aborigine's world. The piercing questions, the sneers and jibes are just as often posed by our own as by whites. Yet I cherish my identity. Black I am; black I will ever be. As long as there are Grants — the living blood of old Wongamar — we will be Aborigines, Wiradjuri. A Chinese friend once told me that home is the last stop on your ancestors' journey; my ancestors' footsteps have travelled for a hundred thousand years across my land to bring me to this point. Where I end, so will my children begin. I hope that when they are older there is enough Aborigine still in me — in them — so that I too can come to my sons in their dreams and ask them, 'Are you ready to become men?'

Bibliography

Ahearne, J., *Michel de Certeau: Interpretation and Its Other*, Polity Press, Cambridge, 1995.

Anderson, M., 'Why an embassy', Australian Institute of Aboriginal and Torres Strait Islander Studies (AIATSIS), PMS 5101, 1972.

Austin, J., and Dodson, M., 'What it means to be black in small country towns', *Identity*, 1974, vol. 2, no. 2, pp. 35–37.

Austin, T., 'Cecil Cook, scientific thought and "half-castes" in the Northern Territory 1927–1939', *Aboriginal History*, 1990, vol. 14, no. 1, pp. 104–122.

Attwood, B. (ed.), *In the Age of Mabo: History, Aborigines and Australia*, Allen & Unwin, St Leonards, NSW, 1996.

Attwood, B., 'Portrait of an Aboriginal as an artist: Sally Morgan and the construction of Aboriginality', *Australian Historical Studies*, 1992, vol. 25, no. 99, pp. 302–318.

Baldwin, J., *The Evidence of Things Not Seen*, Henry Holt and Company, New York, 1995.
Baldwin, J., *The Fire Next Time*, Penguin Books, Harmondsworth, Middlesex, 1964.
Baldwin, J., *Nobody Knows My Name: More Notes of a Native Son*, Corgi Books, London, 1965.
Bandler, F., and Fox, L. (eds), *The Time Was Ripe: A History of the Aboriginal–Australian Fellowship (1956–69)*, Alternative Publishing Co-operative, Chippendale, NSW, 1983.
Barkan, E., *The Guilt of Nations: Restitution and Negotiating Historical Injustices*, W.W. Norton & Company, New York, 2000.
Bayley, W.A., *Down the Lachlan Years Ago: History of Condobolin*, New South Wales, Condobolin Municipal Council, NSW, 1965.
Bennett, S., *White Politics and Black Australians*, Allen & Unwin, St Leonards, NSW, 1999.
Berndt, R.M., 'Wuradjeri magic and "clever men"', *Oceania*, 1947, vol. 17, no. 4, pp. 327–365.
Blainey, G., *The Triumph of the Nomads: A History of Ancient Australia*, Macmillan, Melbourne, 1975.
Brien, C.F. and N.W., *The Brien Family Irish Origins*, D.A.P. for C. Brien and N. Brien, Dubbo, NSW, 1987.
Briscoe, G., 'Aborigines and class in Australian history', Thesis (B.A. (Hons)), Australian National University, Canberra, AIATSIS, MS 2144, 1986.

Broome, R., *Aboriginal Australians: Black Responses to White Dominance, 1788–1980*, Allen & Unwin, St Leonards, NSW, 1982.

Cameron, K., 'Looking back', unpublished, 2000.

Carson, C., Garrow, D.J., and Hine, D.C. (eds), *The Eyes on the Prize Civil Rights Reader*, Penguin Books, New York, 1991.

Cathcart, M., *Manning Clark's History of Australia* (abridged), Melbourne University Press, Melbourne, 1993.

Certeau, M. de (transl. T. Conley), *The Writing of History*, Columbia University Press, New York, 1988.

Chesterman, J., and Galligan, B., *Citizens Without Rights: Aborigines and Australian Citizenship*, Cambridge University Press, Melbourne, 1997.

Clarke, J.H., Bailey, A.P., and Grant, E. (eds), *Malcolm X: The Man and His Times*, Collier Books, New York, 1969.

Clayton, I., 'Warengesda [sic] births, deaths and marriages', Canberra, AIATSIS, PMS 4577, 1988.

Cowlishaw, G., *Rednecks, Eggheads and Blackfellas: A Study of Racial Power and Intimacy in Australia*, Allen & Unwin, St Leonards, NSW, 1999.

Cowlishaw, G., and Morris, B. (eds), *Race Matters: Indigenous Australians and 'Our' Society*, Aboriginal Studies Press, Canberra, 1997.

Curthoys, A., and Markus, A. (eds), *Who Are Our Enemies? Racism and the Australian Working Class*, Hale & Iremonger in association with the Australian Society for the Study of Labour History, Neutral Bay, NSW, 1978.

Davis, F.J., *Who Is Black? One Nation's Definition*, Pennsylvania State University Press, University Park, Pennsylvania, 1991.

D'Souza, D., *The End of Racism: Principles for a Multiracial Society*, Free Press, New York, 1995.

Dyson, M.E., *I May Not Get There With You: The True Martin Luther King, Jr.*, Free Press, New York, 2000.

Dyson, M.E., *Reflecting Black: African–American Cultural Criticism*, University of Minnesota Press, Minneapolis, Minnesota, 1993.

Elphick, B.P, *Riverina Aboriginals: 1874–1945*, D.J. & B.P. Elphick, Canberra, 1997.

Fink, R., 'The caste barrier: An obstacle to the assimilation of part-Aborigines in the north-west of New South Wales', *Oceania*, 1957, vol. 28, no. 2., pp. 100–110.

Fisk, E.K., *The Aboriginal Economy in Town and Country*, George Allen & Unwin, Sydney, and Australian Institute of Aboriginal Studies, Canberra, 1985.

Genovese, E.D., *Roll, Jordan, Roll: The World the Slaves Made*, Vintage Books, New York, 1976.

Gilbert, K.J., *Because a White Man'll Never Do It*, Angus & Robertson, Sydney, 1973.

Gilbert, K.J., *Living Black: Blacks Talk to Kevin Gilbert*, Penguin Books Australia, Ringwood, Vic, 1978.

Goodall, H., *Invasion to Embassy: Land in Aboriginal Politics in New South Wales, 1770–1972*, Allen & Unwin in association with Black Books, St Leonards, NSW, 1996.

Goodall, H., 'Land in our own country: The Aboriginal land rights movement in south eastern Australia, 1860–1914', *Aboriginal History*, 1990, vol. 14., no. 1., pp. 1–24.

Grant, C., *The Cec Grant/Wongamar Story*, The Teachers' Collection, Wagga Wagga, NSW, 1996.

Grant, J., *Providence: The Life and Times of John Grant (1792–1866)*, J. Grant, Orange, NSW, 1994.

Grassby, A.J., and Hill, M., *Six Australian Battlefields: The Black Resistance to Invasion and the White Stuggle Against Colonial Oppression*, Angus & Robertson, North Ryde, NSW, 1988.

Gribble, Rev. E.R.B., 'Warangesda', AIATSIS, PMS 5383, 1900.

Gribble, Rev. J.B., 'Collected papers, 1873–1905', AIATSIS, MS 1514, 1982.

Gresser, P.J, 'The Aborigines of the Bathurst district (historical sketch)', AIATSIS, MS 21 (21/3 a, b), 1965.

Hardy, F., *The Unlucky Australians*, Nelson, Melbourne, 1968.

Harris, A., *Settlers and Convicts, or, Recollections of Sixteen Years' Labour in the Australian Backwoods by an Emigrant Mechanic*, G. Cox, London, 1847.

Hughes, R., *The Fatal Shore: A History of the Transportation of Convicts to Australia 1787–1868*, Pan Books in association with Collins, London, 1988.

Kabaila, P.R., *Wiradjuri Places*, vols 1, 2 and 3, Black Mountain Projects, Jamison Centre, ACT, 1995–1998.

Keed, R., *Memories of Bulgandramine Mission*, R. Keed, Peak Hill, NSW, 1985.

Kelly, R., *Paradise Divided: The Changes, the Challenges, the Choices for Australia*, Allen & Unwin, St Leonards, NSW, 2000.

Kubank, L.A., 'The Warangesda Mission', AIATSIS, PMS 5382, 1900.

Langton, M., '"Well, I heard it on the radio and I saw it on the television": An essay for the Australian Film Commission on the politics and aesthetics of filmmaking by and about Aboriginal people and things', Australian Film Commission, North Sydney, NSW, 1993.

Levine, L.W., *Black Culture and Black Consciousness: Afro–American Folk Thought from Slavery to Freedom*, Oxford University Press, New York, 1977.

McGrath, M.A., 'John Brown Gribble: The friend of the blackfellow', Thesis (B.Lett.), Australian National University, Canberra, AIATSIS, MS 3030, 1989.

McGregor, A., *Cathy Freeman: A Journey Just Begun*, Random House Australia, Milsons Point, NSW, 1998.

McGregor, R., 'Protest and progress: Aboriginal activism in the 1930s', *Australian Historical Studies*, 1993, vol. 25, no. 101, pp. 555–568.

Malcomson, S.L., *One Drop of Blood: The American Misadventure of Race*, Farrar, Straus and Giroux, New York, 2000.

Manne, R.M., *In Denial: The Stolen Generations and the Right*, Schwartz Publishing, Melbourne, 2001.

Marable, M., *Beyond Black and White: Transforming African– American Politics*, Verso, London and New York, 1995.

Markus, A., *From the Barrel of a Gun: The Oppression of the Aborigines, 1860–1900*, Victorian Historical Association, West Melbourne, Vic, 1974.

Markus, A., *Race: John Howard and the Remaking of Australia*, Allen & Unwin, Crows Nest, NSW, 2001.

Mason, S.L., 'The textual construction of Aboriginal identity in late twentieth century Australia', Thesis (B.A. (Hons)), University of Adelaide, Adelaide, AIATSIS, MS 2758, 1989.

Moore, L., and Williams, S., *The True Story of Jimmy Governor*, Allen & Unwin, Crows Nest, NSW, 2001.

Orwell, G., *Inside the Whale and Other Essays*, Penguin Books, Harmondsworth, Middlesex, 1957.

Pakenham, T., *The Year of Liberty: The Great Irish Rebellion of 1798*, Abacus, London, 2000.

Pearson, M., 'Bathurst Plains and beyond: European colonisation and Aboriginal resistance', Aboriginal History, 1984, vol. 8, no. 1, pp. 63–79.

Perkins, C., *A Bastard Like Me*, Ure Smith, Sydney, 1975.

Read, P., 'A history of Erambie Mission, Cowra, prepared for the NSW Select Committee into Aboriginal Welfare', Canberra, AIATSIS, PMS 31, 1979.

Read, P., 'A history of the Wiradjuri people of New South Wales, 1883–1969', Thesis (Ph. D.), Australian National University, Canberra, AIATSIS, MS 1850, 1983.

Read, P., '"A rape of the soul so profound": Some reflections on the dispersal policy in New South Wales', *Aboriginal History*, 1983, vol. 7, no. 1, pp. 23–33.

Read, P., '"Breaking up these camps entirely": The dispersal policy in Wiradjuri country 1909–1929', *Aboriginal History*, 1984, vol. 8, no. 1, pp. 45–55.

Reece, B., 'Inventing Aborigines', *Aboriginal History*, 1987, vol. 11, no. 1, pp. 14–23.

Reynolds, H., *Aboriginal Sovereignty: Reflections on Race, State and Nation*, Allen & Unwin, St Leonards, NSW, 1996.

Reynolds, H. (ed.), *Dispossession: Black Australians and White Invaders*, Allen & Unwin, Sydney, 1989.

Reynolds, H., *Frontier: Aborigines, Settlers and Land*, Allen & Unwin, Sydney, 1987.

Reynolds, H., 'Jimmy Governor and Jimmie Blacksmith', *Australian Literary Studies*, 1979, vol. 9, no. 1, pp. 14–25.

Reynolds, H., *This Whispering in Our Hearts*, Allen & Unwin, St Leonards, NSW, 1998.

Roberts, D., 'Bells Falls massacre and Bathurst's history of violence: Local tradition and Australian historiography', *Australian Historical Studies*, 1995, vol. 26, no. 105, pp. 615–633.

Robinson, S., and Strachan, L., 'The Aboriginal embassy: An account of the protests of 1972', *Aboriginal History*, 1994, vol. 18, no. 1, pp. 49–63.

Robinson, S., and Strachan, L., 'The Aboriginal embassy, 1972', Thesis (M.A.), Australian National University, Canberra, AIATSIS, MS 3184, 1993.

Rowley, C.D., *Outcasts in White Australia*, Australian National University Press, Canberra, 1971.

Rowley, C.D., *The Destruction of Aboriginal Society*, Penguin Books Australia, Ringwood, Vic, 1972.

Salisbury, T., and Gresser, P.J., *Windradyne of the Wiradjuri: Martial Law at Bathurst in 1824*, Wentworth Books, Sydney, 1971.

Sandall, R., *The Culture Cult: Designer Tribalism and Other Essays*, Westview Press, Boulder, Colorado, 2001.

Sharrock, D., and Devenport, M., *Man of War, Man of Peace? The Unauthorised Biography of Gerry Adams*, Macmillan, London, 1997.

Skocpol, T., *States and Social Revolutions: A Comparative Analysis of France, Russia and China*, Cambridge University Press, Cambridge, 1979.

Stanner, W.E.H., *After the Dreaming*, ABC Enterprises for the Australian Broadcasting Corporation, Crows Nest, NSW, 1991.

Stanner, W.E.H., 'The history of indifference thus begins', *Aboriginal History*, 1977, vol. 1, no. 1, pp. 3–26.

Suttor, W.H., *Australian Stories Retold, and, Sketches of Country Life*, Glyndwr Whalan, Bathurst, NSW, 1887.

Swain, T., and Rose, D.B. (eds), *Aboriginal Australians and Christian Missions: Ethnographic and Historical Studies*, Australian Association for the Study of Religions, Bedford Park, SA, 1988.

Sykes, R., 'Blacks Will Get Blacker This Year', *Nation Review*, 5–11 January 1973, pp. 366–367.

Thompson, E.P., *The Making of the English Working Class*, Penguin Books, Harmondsworth, Middlesex, 1963.

Tickner, R., *Taking a Stand: Land Rights to Reconciliation*, Allen & Unwin, Crows Nest, NSW, 2001.

Torres, R.D., Miron, L.F. and Inda, J.X. (eds), *Race, Identity, and Citizenship: A Reader*, Blackwell Publishers, Malden, Massachusetts, 1999.

[Unknown], *The Life and Adventures of Jeremiah Grant*, James Duffy, Dublin, 1842.

Walker, C., *Buried Country: The Story of Aboriginal Country Music*, Pluto Press, Sydney, 2000.

Windschuttle, K., *The Killing of History: How Literary Critics and Social Theorists Are Murdering Our Past*, Encounter Books, San Francisco, 2000.

Woolmington, J., 'Wellington Valley in 1835: A house divided against itself', *Push from the Bush*, 1983, vol. 16, pp. 24–32.

JOURNALS

Grant, J., 'Diary', unpublished, 1904.

Gribble, Rev. J.B., 'Journal: Early days at Yarrabah 1891–1892' (incomplete), State Library of New South Wales, ML MSS 4503.

Gunther, J., 'Journal,1836–1866', State Library of New South Wales, 1838.

'Warangesda Mission manager's diary, 18 March 1887 to 11 April 1897', Darlington Point, NSW, AIATSIS, MS 1786, 1887–1897.

NEWSPAPERS AND PERIODICALS

Aborigines' Friends' Association Annual Report 1961.

Dawn: A Magazine for the Aboriginal People of NSW, New South Wales Aborigines Welfare Board, Sydney, March 1967; November/ December 1977.

Identity, Aboriginal Publications Foundation, Canberra.

Our A.I.M., The Mission, West Maitland, NSW, January 1909; December 1909; May 1914; March 1919; April 1919; May 1919; June 1919; December 1919; July 1921; September 1921; October 1921; September 1922; July 1929; October 1929; April 1932.
The Age.
The Area News, Griffith, NSW.
The Australian.
The Australian Abo Call: The Voice of the Aborigines, Sydney.
The Canberra Times.
The Daily Telegraph.
The Gundagai Times.
The Koorier, Fitzroy, Vic.
The Sydney Morning Herald.
The Washington Post.

HOUSE OF COMMONS SESSIONAL PAPERS
1835 Report from the Select Committee on Aborigines (British Settlement).
1836 Report from the Select Committee on Aborigines (British Settlement).

INTERVIEWS
Alma Cowley, Cowra, 2001.
Chicka Dixon, Sydney, 2001.
Madeleine Forgey, Cowra, 2001.
Don Grant, Sydney, 1999.
Elizabeth Grant, Canberra, 2001.

Graham Grant, Canberra, 2001.
Monsignor Leo Grant, Bathurst, 2001.
Stan Grant senior, Canberra, 2001.
Ivy Jackson, Dubbo, 2001.
Bob McLeod, Nowra, 2001.

TALKING TO MY COUNTRY

Talking to My Country is Stan Grant's very personal meditation on race, identity and history. It is that rare and special book that talks to every Australian about their country – what it is, and what it could be. It is not just about race, or about Indigenous people but all of us, our shared identity. Direct, honest and forthright, Stan is talking to us all. He might not have all the answers but he wants us to keep on asking the question: how can we be better?

> 'an urgent and flowing narrative in a book that should be on the required reading list in every school' – *The Australian*

> 'Grant will be an important voice in shaping this nation' – *The Saturday Paper*

AUSTRALIA DAY

As uncomfortable as it is, we need to reckon with our history. On January 26, no Australian can really look away. There are the hard questions we ask of ourselves on Australia Day.

Since publishing his critically acclaimed, Walkley Award winning, bestselling memoir *Talking to My Country* in early 2016, Stan Grant has been crossing the country, talking to huge crowds everywhere about how racism is at the heart of our history and the Australian dream. But Stan knows this is not where the story ends.

In this book, *Australia Day*, his long-awaited follow up to *Talking to My Country*, Stan talks about our country, about who we are as a nation, about the indigenous struggle for belonging and identity in Australia, and what it means to be Australian. A sad, wise, beautiful, reflective and troubled book, *Australia Day* asks the questions that have to be asked, that no else seems to be asking.

Who are we? What is our country? How do we move forward from here?

> ‘a soulful meditation on who we are by an Australian whose emotional and intellectual range is as vast as the ochreous land itself” – *The Australian*

THE QUEEN IS DEAD

'History is not weighted on the scales, it is felt in our bones. It is worn on our skin. It is scarred in memory.'

The Queen reigned for seventy years. She came to the throne at the height of Empire and died with the world at a tipping point. What comes next after the death of what Stan Grant calls 'the last white Queen'?

From one of our most respected and award-winning journalists, Stan Grant, *The Queen is Dead* is a searing, viscerally powerful, emotionally unstoppable, pull-no-punches book on the bitter legacy of colonialism for indigenous people. Taking us on a journey through the world's fault lines, from the war in Ukraine, the rise of China, the identity wars, the resurgence of white supremacy, and the demand that Black Lives Matter, *The Queen is Dead* is a full-throated, impassioned argument on the necessity for an end to monarchy in Australia, the need for a Republic, and what needs to be done - through the Voice to Parliament and beyond - to address and redress the pain and sorrow and humiliations of the past.

Momentous and timely, *The Queen is Dead* carries an urgent, undeniable and righteous demand for justice, for a reckoning, and a just settlement with First Nations people.